Microsoft Excel It!

Teen-based Microsoft Excel Activities

First Edition

David Salem
Joy Tavano

BUSINESS EDUCATION PUBLISHING™

www.bepublishing.com

Copyright

Microsoft Excel It!
Published by Business Education Publishing

Authors
David Salem
Joy Tavano

Editors
Michael Gecawich
Kathleen Hicks
Monica Handy
Diane Silvia
Linda Viveiros
Lisa Wardle

Student Reviewers
Dan Dowding
Bill Nardone

ISBN: 0-9774611-0-6

Permissions
For permission to use materials from this text, please contact us by:

Tel: 888.781.6921
Fax: 401.781.7608
Web: www.bepublishing.com

Business Education Publishing
Box 8558 • Warwick, RI 02888 • U.S.A.

INTRODUCTION

Welcome to *Microsoft Excel It!*, the first in a new series of Microsoft Office activity books published by Business Education Publishing. The *It!* (Information Technology) series provides students with practice activities to help them become proficient users of the Microsoft Office software applications suite.

Microsoft Excel It! provides students with teen-based practice activities to help them apply real-world data to Microsoft Excel spreadsheets. Completing the activities in this book will prepare students for the Microsoft Office Specialist Certification in Excel.

Prerequisite Skills Required
The student should have a basic working knowledge of Microsoft Excel software. This textbook does not provide step-by-step instructions specific to any one particular version of Microsoft Excel; rather, it provides general instructions for students to practice using any version of Microsoft Excel.

Compatibility
The instructions have been written for any version of Microsoft Excel running on a Windows operating system. However, with small modifications, this book can easily be used with Macintosh-based systems.

Standards
The skills in this book align with NBEA (*National Business Education Association*) and ISTE (*International Society for Technology Education*) information technology standards for spreadsheets.

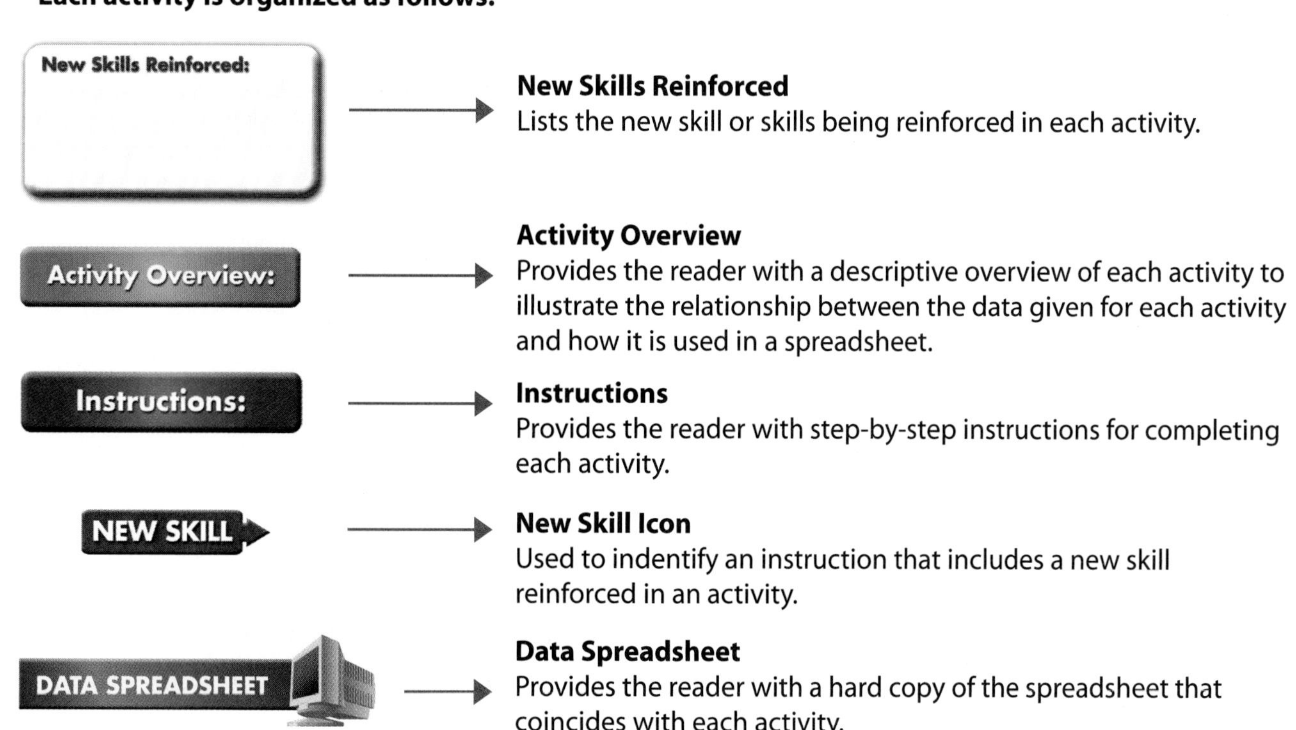

Organization of the Textbook

The text is organized into a hierarchical skill-level format. With a few exceptions, most of the activities in the book build upon skills practiced in previous activities.

Each activity is organized as follows:

New Skills Reinforced
Lists the new skill or skills being reinforced in each activity.

Activity Overview
Provides the reader with a descriptive overview of each activity to illustrate the relationship between the data given for each activity and how it is used in a spreadsheet.

Instructions
Provides the reader with step-by-step instructions for completing each activity.

New Skill Icon
Used to indentify an instruction that includes a new skill reinforced in an activity.

Data Spreadsheet
Provides the reader with a hard copy of the spreadsheet that coincides with each activity.

SKILLS REINFORCED IN EACH ACTIVITY

The table below provides the new skills reinforced in each activity in the book.

Activity #	Title	New Skills Reinforced
1.	Search Engines	• Enter data in a spreadsheet • Identify cell addresses • Save a spreadsheet • Set the print area of a spreadsheet
2.	American Top 40 Music	• Align cell data to left, right, and center • Print preview
3.	Online Activities	• Change font size • Use bold, italics, and underline text-style enhancements
4.	San Antonio Spurs®	• Change column widths
5.	FBLA Club Members	• Format cells to text • Sort data in ascending order
6.	Internet Advertisers	• Use the AutoFill feature to complete a number sequence
7.	Abercrombie & Fitch®	• Format cells as numbers
8.	FBLA Club Members 2	• Retrieve a stored file • Save an existing file using a different name • Change page orientation to landscape
9.	Movie Release Dates	• Format cells as dates
10.	S.A.T. Scores	• Add numbers using a formula • Use the AutoFill feature to complete formulas • Display formulas
11.	S.A.T. Scores 2	• Use Average, Maximum, and Minimum • Sort data in descending order
12.	Gap® Payroll Register	• Use formulas to multiply, add, and subtract numbers • Use parentheses in formulas • Use a formula that references the answer to another cell's formula • Change page margins
13.	NHL® Standings	• Print gridlines • Copy and paste formulas
14.	Chicago White Sox®	• Divide numbers in a formula • Increase a cell's decimal places • Use the SUM function
15.	Best Buy®	• Format row height
16.	Circuit City®	• Insert a page header
17.	Celebrity Searches	• Merge cells • Insert a page footer

SKILLS REINFORCED IN EACH ACTIVITY

Activity #	Title	New Skills Reinforced
18.	Fast Food Nutrition	• Format text direction
19.	Concerts	• Change column widths using AutoFit • Format cells as currency
20.	Reality TV	• Use text wrap within cells
21.	Candy Holidays	• Insert a clipart image in a spreadsheet
22.	Astrology	• Insert comments for cells
23.	Xbox 360®	• Format cells to currency using the dollar sign button on the formatting toolbar
24.	Music Store Checkbook	• Use the AutoSum button on the standard toolbar
25.	Sales Report	• None. This activity provides additional reinforcement in using many of the skills introduced in previous activities.
26.	Accounts Payable	• Format cells to percents
27.	San Antonio Spurs® 2	• Cut, copy, and paste data • Use sets of parentheses in formulas
28.	Quarterback Statistics	• Change cell shading
29.	Recipes	• Format cells as fractions
30.	NBA® Standings	• Insert and delete rows
31.	Old Navy® Sales	• Use the absolute cell reference in a formula
32.	Amazon.com® Music	• Format font colors
33.	Top 10 DVDs	• Insert columns • Move columns
34.	Expense Report	• Insert a page break
35.	Personal CD Collection	• Delete columns • Use <CTRL>+D to duplicate data in cells
36.	Careers	• Adjust page scaling
37.	Fidelity Investments®	• Format cells to negative numbers • Change a cell's fill color
38.	Abercrombie & Fitch® 2	• Use the Count function • Use the AutoFormat feature
39.	Music Genres	• Import a text file into Excel • Use cell borders

SKILLS REINFORCED IN EACH ACTIVITY

Activity #	Title	New Skills Reinforced
40.	Chicago White Sox® 2	• Print a spreadsheet with row and column headings
41.	Yearly Earnings	• Freeze panes
42.	Teen Cars	• Insert WordArt in a spreadsheet • Edit and format WordArt
43.	TV Show Standings	• Insert a line from the drawing toolbar
44.	Student Travel	• Format cells as accounting • Apply borders to a cell range
45.	American Idol®	• Create a pie chart • Enhance charts by changing colors and font sizes
46.	iTunes®	• Create a column chart
47.	X Games®	• Create a line chart • Select cells using multiple ranges • Use the Fill Effects feature in a chart
48.	MTV®	• Create a bar chart • Align text in a chart
49.	Raise	• Use conditions in formulas
50.	Teacher's Grade Book	• Use the Median and Mode functions • Use multiple conditions in formulas
51.	NBA® Standings 2	• Expand on the use of the absolute cell reference in formulas
52.	Mortgage Calculator	• Use the Payment (PMT) function
53.	529 College Savings	• Use the Future Value (FV) function
54.	NFL® Fantasy Football®	• Use the ROUNDDOWN function
55.	Computer Games	• Rename worksheets • Use multiple worksheets • Use Paste Link formulas
56.	Comic Books	• Create an exploded pie chart
57.	Who Got Punk'D®?	• Combine cells
58.	Monthly Calendar	• Use a spreadsheet to create a monthly calendar
59.	Prom Expenses	• Format a business letter using Microsoft Word • Insert an Excel spreadsheet into a Microsoft Word document
60.	College Choices	• Use a spreadsheet as a database to store and organize data

TABLE OF CONTENTS

ACTIVITY 1: SEARCH ENGINES

New Skills Reinforced:

In this activity, you will practice how to:

1. enter data in a spreadsheet.
2. identify cell addresses by placing the cursor in a specified cell address.
3. save a spreadsheet.
4. set the print area of a spreadsheet.

Activity Overview:

The Web is a rich source for current local, national, and international news. There are millions of Web sites on the World Wide Web, from broadcast sources to newspapers. There are several search engines available for Web searches. Users must type in keywords or phrases related to the topic to be researched. For an effective search, it is best to enter multiple search terms or phrases related to the subject of interest. The more precise you are with the keywords or phrases, the better the results.

The following activity illustrates how spreadsheets can be used to log data to track search engine results. In this spreadsheet, the percentage of people using the top five search engines in July and August 2005 are provided, along with the change in percentage from July to August.

Instructions:

1. Create a NEW spreadsheet.

   Note: Unless otherwise stated, the font should be set to Arial, the font size to 10 point.

2. NEW SKILL Type the data as shown. Notice how the cell address changes with each new entry.
3. Carefully proofread your work for accuracy.
4. NEW SKILL Save the spreadsheet as SEARCH ENGINES.
5. NEW SKILL Set the Print Area of the spreadsheet to include cells A1 – G12.
6. Print a copy of the spreadsheet if required by your instructor.

ACTIVITY 1: SEARCH ENGINES DATA SPREADSHEET

	A	B	C	D	E	F	G
1	Activity 1 Student Name						
2	Top 5 Search Engines Ranked by Search Share, July-August 2005 (%)						
3							
4							
5							
6							
7	Ranking		Provider		July	August	Change
8	1		Google		44.7	45.9	1.2
9	2		Yahoo!		21.8	23.2	1.4
10	3		MSN		12.2	11.4	-0.8
11	4		AOL		8.4	8	-0.4
12	5		Ask Jeeves		1.6	2.1	0.5

Source: http://www.clickz.com/stats/sectors/search_tools/article.php/3554731

ACTIVITY 2: AMERICAN TOP 40 MUSIC

New Skills Reinforced:

In this activity, you will practice how to:

1. align cell data to left, right, and center positions.
2. print preview to adjust setup so the spreadsheet fits on one page.

Activity Overview:

AT40.com is a music Web site where people can see the latest top ten songs of the week in addition to obtaining information about various music artists. The top ten songs of the week are listed as well as the previous week's (last week) top ten ranking for the same songs. The top ten fan picks are also listed. American Top 40 also provides its Web site visitors with detailed entertainment news.

The following activity illustrates how spreadsheets can be used to organize fan picks as well as the top ten songs of the current and the previous week. In this activity, you will be practicing how to align data in columns to make the spreadsheet easier to read.

Instructions:

1. Create a NEW spreadsheet.

   Note: Unless otherwise stated, the font should be set to Arial, the font size to 10 point.

2. Type the data as shown.
3. NEW SKILL ▸ Center align the data in cells A6 – B18.
4. NEW SKILL ▸ Right align the data in cells C7 – C18.
5. NEW SKILL ▸ Left align the data in cells D8 – F18.
6. Carefully proofread your work for accuracy.
7. Save the spreadsheet as AMERICAN TOP 40 MUSIC.
8. Analyze the changes made to the data in the spreadsheet.
9. Set the Print Area to include all cells containing data in the spreadsheet.
10. NEW SKILL ▸ Print Preview and adjust the Page Setup so that the spreadsheet fits on one page.
11. Print a copy of the spreadsheet if required by your instructor.

	A	B	C	D	E	F	G	H	I
1	Activity 2 Student Name								
2	AT40.com MUSIC								
3									
4	TOP SONGS OF THE WEEK NOVEMBER 11, 2005								
5									
6	RANK	RANK							
7	THIS	LAST	FAN						
8	WEEK	WEEK	PICKS	ARTIST		SONG			
9	1	1	3	Kanye West		Gold Digger			
10	2	2	1	Kelly Clarkson		Because of You			
11	3	6	2	Nickelback		Photograph			
12	4	3	5	Mariah Carey		Shake it off			
13	5	5	4	Black Eyed Peas		My Humps			
14	6	7	6	Chris Brown		Run It			
15	7	8	7	Fall Out Boy		Sugar We're Goin' Down			
16	8	4	8	Green Day		Wake Me Up When September Ends			
17	9	9	10	Bow Wow		Like You			
18	10	10	9	Weezer		Beverly Hills			

Source: AT40.com

ACTIVITY 3: ONLINE ACTIVITIES

New Skills Reinforced:

In this activity, you will practice how to:
1. change font size.
2. use bold, italics, and underline text-style enhancements.

Activity Overview:

More teenagers are going online and doing more things online than they did in previous years. A new "Teens and Technology" report from Pew Internet and American Life found that 87 percent of American teens ages 12 to 17 used the Internet in 2004, up from 73 percent in 2000. The frequency of teens' online usage has also risen 51 percent since that time, and the number of teens who report they go online daily is up from 42 percent in 2000. The report also found 51 percent of online teens live in homes with broadband Internet access.

Teens now use a broader array of online content and services. E-mail is still the number one activity while visits to entertainment Web sites are popular as well. Teens going online to play games, check news, make purchases, and get health information is also on the rise. In comparison with adults, teens play more online games, Instant Message more, and have a higher propensity to go online to get news on current events.

The following activity illustrates how spreadsheets can be used to compare online activities of teens versus adults.

Instructions:

1. Create a NEW spreadsheet.

   Note: Unless otherwise stated, the font should be set to Arial, the font size to 10 point.

2. Type the data as shown.

NEW SKILL

3. Apply the following text enhancements:
   a. Bold cell A2 and change the font size to 14 point.
   b. Bold cells F8 and H8.
   c. Bold and underline cells A9, F9, and H9.
   d. Italicize cells A26 – A29.
4. Center align cells F8 – F19 and H8 – H19.
5. Carefully proofread your work for accuracy.
6. Save the spreadsheet as ONLINE ACTIVITIES.
7. Analyze the changes made to the data in the spreadsheet.
8. Set the Print Area to include all cells containing data in the spreadsheet.
9. Print Preview and adjust the Page Setup so that the spreadsheet fits on one page.
10. Print a copy of the spreadsheet if required by your instructor.

ACTIVITY 3: ONLINE ACTIVITIES DATA SPREADSHEET

	A	B	C	D	E	F	G	H	I
1	Activity 3 Student Name								
2	Likelihood of Teen and Adult Engagement in Online Activities								
3	October - November 2004 survey								
4									
5									
6									
7									
8						(%)		(%)	
9	Activity Description					Online Teens		Online Adults	
10	Play online games					81		32	
11	Send or receive Instant Messages					75		42	
12	Get information about a school you might attend					57		45	
13	Send or read e-mail					89		90	
14	Get news or information about current events					76		73	
15	Look for news about politics					55		58	
16	Look for religious or spiritual information					26		30	
17	Buy things, such as books, clothing, or music					43		67	
18	Look for health, dieting, or fitness information					31		66	
19	Look for information about a job					30		44	
20									
21									
22									
23									
24									
25	Notes:								
26	1. Margin of error is 4% for online teens.								
27	2. Margin of error is 3% for online adults for all surveys except for November 2004, which is 5%.								
28	3. Teen data is from an October-November 2004 survey.								
29	4. Adult data is from a December 2002 survey and a November 2004-January 2005 survey.								

Source: http://www.clickz.com/stats/sectors/demographics/article.php/3523376

ACTIVITY 4: SAN ANTONIO SPURS®

New Skills Reinforced:

In this activity, you will practice how to:

1. change column widths to ensure cell data fits properly in columns.

Activity Overview:

The San Antonio Spurs® are the 2004-2005 National Basketball Association® (NBA®) champions. In the 2005 NBA® Finals, the Spurs® defeated the defending champion, the Detroit Pistons®, in a thrilling seventh game. Led by their perennial All-Star Tim Duncan, the NBA's® MVP in 2002 and 2003, and head coach Greg Popovich, the San Antonio Spurs® have won three NBA® Championships (1999, 2003, 2005).

The Spurs are the only major professional sports franchise to be located in the San Antonio area. The city shares a unique bond with the team, and the Spurs'® players are active members of the San Antonio community. The San Antonio Spurs® are frequently ranked as one of the top U.S. sports franchises by fans.

The following activity illustrates how spreadsheets can be used to create a sports roster that lists the team's players, uniform numbers, positions, and the number of games played.

Instructions:

1. Create a NEW spreadsheet.

   Note: Unless otherwise stated, the font should be set to Arial, the font size to 10 point.

2. Type the data as shown.
3. Bold cell A2 and change the font size to 20 point.
4. Bold cell A3 and change the font size to 14 point.
5. Bold cells A4, B8 – D8, and A9 – D9.
6. **NEW SKILL** Format the width of column A to 20.0.
7. **NEW SKILL** Format the width of columns B, C, and D to 10.0 and center align.
8. Carefully proofread your work for accuracy.
9. Save the spreadsheet as SAN ANTONIO SPURS.
10. Analyze the changes made to the data in the spreadsheet.
11. Set the Print Area to include all cells containing data in the spreadsheet.
12. Print Preview and adjust the Page Setup so that the spreadsheet fits on one page.
13. Print a copy of the spreadsheet if required by your instructor.

ACTIVITY 4: SAN ANTONIO SPURS® DATA SPREADSHEET

	A	B	C	D
1	Activity 4 Student Name			
2	N.B.A. CHAMPIONS			
3	SAN ANTONIO SPURS			
4	2004-05 Roster			
5				
6	Head Coach: Greg Popovich			
7				
8		JERSEY	POSITION	GAMES
9	PLAYER	NUMBER	PLAYED	PLAYED
10				
11	Tim Duncan	21	F, C	66
12	Tony Parker	9	G	80
13	Manu Ginobili	20	G	74
14	Glenn Robinson	3	F	9
15	Bruce Bowen	12	F	82
16	Brent Barry	17	G	81
17	Devin Brown	23	G	67
18	Nazr Mohammed	2	C	23
19	Robert Horry	5	F, C	75
20	Beno Udrih	14	G	80
21	Rasho Nesterovic	8	C	70
22	Dion Glover	9	G, F	7
23	Sean Marks	40	F, C	23
24	Tony Massenburg	34	F, C	61
25	Mike Wilks	29	G	48
26	Linton Johnson III	43	F	2

Source: http://aol.nba.com/spurs/stats/2004/index.html

ACTIVITY 5: FBLA CLUB MEMBERS

New Skills Reinforced:

In this activity, you will practice how to:
1. format cells to text.
2. sort data in ascending order (A–Z).

Activity Overview:

Future Business Leaders of America-Phi Beta Lambda (FBLA-PBL) is a non-profit education association of students preparing for careers in business and business-related fields. The Association has four divisions:

1. FBLA for high school students
2. FBLA Middle Level for junior high, middle, and intermediate school students
3. PBL for postsecondary students
4. Professional Alumni Division for business people, educators, and parents who support the goals of the Association

The FBLA-PBL's mission is to bring business and education together in a positive working relationship through innovative leadership and career development programs. FBLA-PBL is headquartered in Reston, Virginia, and is organized on local, state, and national levels. Business teachers/advisors and advisory councils (including school officials, business people, and community representatives) guide local chapters. State advisors and committee members coordinate chapter activities for the national organization.

The following activity illustrates how spreadsheets can be used to list club members and then alphabetize them.

Note: *The names in this activity are not actual students or instructors at Alamo Heights High School.*

Instructions:

1. Create a NEW spreadsheet.
   Note: Unless otherwise stated, the font should be set to Arial, the font size to 10 point.
2. Type the data as shown.
3. Bold cells A2 and A6.
4. Bold and underline cells B9 – E9.
5. NEW SKILL ▶ Select all cells (*Shortcut: <CTRL> + A*) and format cells to text.
6. Format the width of column A to 6.0 and left align.
7. Format the width of columns B and C to 16.0 and left align.
8. Format the width of column D to 10.0 and center align.
9. Format the width of column E to 14.0 and left align.
10. NEW SKILL ▶ To alphabetize students by their last names, select cells B10 – E29 and sort in ascending order (A–Z). Use the column labeled "LAST" to Sort by.
11. Carefully proofread your work for accuracy.
12. Save the spreadsheet as FBLA CLUB MEMBERS.
13. Analyze the changes made to the data in the spreadsheet.
14. Set the Print Area to include all cells containing data in the spreadsheet.
15. Print Preview and adjust the Page Setup so that the spreadsheet fits on one page.
16. Print a copy of the spreadsheet if required by your instructor.

ACTIVITY 5: FBLA CLUB MEMBERS DATA SPREADSHEET

	A	B	C	D	E
1	Activity 5 Student Name				
2	ALAMO Heights High School				
3	6900 Broadway				
4	San Antonio, Texas 78209				
5					
6	Future Business Leaders of America (FBLA) Club Members 2006-07				
7	Advisor: Lea Meyers				
8					
9		LAST	FIRST	ID #	YEAR
10		Liang	Shun Yi	3771	Senior
11		Zhou	Xuyang	2278	Sophomore
12		Jefferson	Henry	3996	Sophomore
13		Soares	Candace	9745	Freshman
14		Wong	Miao Xian	4533	Sophomore
15		Forsyth	Amanda	4322	Junior
16		Nemenko	Ashley	6125	Senior
17		Huang	Sze Wai	7957	Senior
18		Chan	Zhu Na	1988	Senior
19		Moses	Shani	2289	Sophomore
20		Khazanovich	Karina	0155	Freshman
21		Hudson	Dana	5044	Freshman
22		Tinaz	Murat	7109	Freshman
23		Chung	Marvin	3229	Junior
24		Tan	Joanna	6894	Junior
25		Chu	Jason	3680	Freshman
26		Leung	Jenny	0960	Junior
27		Frederic	Rashida	1526	Senior
28		St. Fleur	Fadhylla	9509	Freshman
29		Chao	Hao Ting	9978	Sophomore

Source: http://www.fbla-pbl.org/

ACTIVITY 6: INTERNET ADVERTISERS

New Skills Reinforced:

In this activity, you will practice how to:

1. use the AutoFill feature to complete a number sequence in a spreadsheet.

Activity Overview:

Media consumption and advertising is spurring excitement differently than it was just a few years ago. Advertisers realize that media now goes hand-in-hand with technology. Internet advertising has been steadily increasing over the past decade and is designed to support communication with consumers. Whether you're an agency or advertiser looking to maximize your investment or a Web publisher targeting prospects, online advertising delivers complete, accurate, and virtually real-time exposure to products and services.

The following activity illustrates how spreadsheets can be used to chart the frequency of advertising by providing a list of the leading Internet advertisers.

Instructions:

1. Create a NEW spreadsheet.

   Note: Unless otherwise stated, the font should be set to Arial, the font size to 10 point.
2. Type the data as shown.
3. Bold cell A2 and change the font size to 20 point.
4. Bold cell A3 and change the font size to 14 point.
5. Bold rows 5 and 6.
6. **NEW SKILL** Use the AutoFill feature to automatically complete the series of POSITION numbers. To do this, select cells A8 – A9. While the cells are selected, click the bottom right-hand corner of cell A9 until the mouse pointer changes to a "+" sign. Now drag the mouse pointer down to cell A32 and release the mouse button. The cells should now be filled to complete the number sequence for cells A8 – A32.
7. Format the width of column A to 12.0 and left align.
8. Center align cells A6 – A32.
9. Format the width of column B to 32.0 and left align.
10. Format the width of columns C and D to 20.0 and center align.
11. Carefully proofread your work for accuracy.
12. Save the spreadsheet as INTERNET ADVERTISERS.
13. Analyze the changes made to the data in the spreadsheet.
14. Set the Print Area to include all cells containing data in the spreadsheet.
15. Print Preview and adjust the Page Setup so that the spreadsheet fits on one page.
16. Print a copy of the spreadsheet if required by your instructor.

ACTIVITY 6: INTERNET ADVERTISERS DATA SPREADSHEET

	A	B	C	D
1	Activity 6 Student Name			
2	Top 25 Internet Advertisers			
3	SEPTEMBER 2005			
4				
5			ADVERTISING	
6	POSITION	ADVERTISER	FREQUENCY	SECTOR
7				
8	1	Vonage	20632	Technology
9	2	Classmates.com	15510	Miscellaneous
10		Ameritrade Brokerage	8355	Finance
11		Superpages.com	6761	Miscellaneous
12		Netflix.com	6413	Entertainment
13		Overstock.com	6369	Retail
14		Amazon.com	5462	Retail
15		Monster.com	5420	Classifieds
16		LowerMyBills.com	5251	Finance
17		RealArcade Games	4698	Entertainment
18		Scottrade Stock Brokerage	4644	Finance
19		Love@AOL	4560	Dating
20		Dell VAR Computers Products Direct	4347	Technology
21		Circuit City	4145	Retail
22		Capital One	4043	Finance
23		University of Phoenix Online	4000	Education
24		Harrisdirect.com	3770	Finance
25		Earthlink	3734	Technology
26		CareerBuilder	3715	Classifieds
27		Freecreditreport.com	3704	Finance
28		eBay.com	3618	Retail
29		Nextag Services	3455	Miscellaneous
30		Viagra RX	3189	Health
31		Devry University	3189	Education
32		Dell Inspiron Computers Direct	3167	Technology

Source: http://www.clickz.com/stats/sectors/advertising/article.php/3562801

ACTIVITY 7: ABERCROMBIE & FITCH®

New Skills Reinforced:

In this activity, you will practice how to:

1. format cells as numbers.

Activity Overview:

Abercrombie & Fitch® is one of the most successful specialty clothing retailers in the world. Their casual, classic, and All-American lifestyle brand of clothing is synonymous with quality. Their target audience is high school and college students across the globe. They purchase their products from quality manufacturers and then sell to consumers at a huge markup.

The following activity illustrates how spreadsheets can be used by a retail clothing store to list the cost of merchandise (unit cost) and its selling price.

Instructions:

1. Create a NEW spreadsheet.

   Note: Unless otherwise stated, the font should be set to Arial, the font size to 10 point.
2. Type the data as shown.
3. Bold cell A2 and change the font size to 14 point.
4. Bold cells A3, A9, and A20.
5. Bold rows 6 and 7.
6. Format the width of column A to 14.0 and left align.
7. Format the width of column B to 14.0 and center align.
8. Format the width of columns C and D to 20.0 and left align.
9. Format the width of columns E and F to 9.0 and center align.
10. NEW SKILL ▶ Select column B and format it as numbers displaying 0 decimal places.
11. NEW SKILL ▶ Select columns E and F and format them as numbers displaying 2 decimal places.
12. Carefully proofread your work for accuracy.
13. Save the spreadsheet as ABERCROMBIE & FITCH.
14. Analyze the changes made to the data in the spreadsheet.
15. Set the Print Area to include all cells containing data in the spreadsheet.
16. Print Preview and adjust the Page Setup so that the spreadsheet fits on one page.
17. Print a copy of the spreadsheet if required by your instructor.

ACTIVITY 7: ABERCROMBIE & FITCH® DATA SPREADSHEET

	A	B	C	D	E	F
1	Activity 7 Student Name					
2	ABERCROMBIE & FITCH					
3	Markup Schedule November 2005					
4						
5						
6		ITEM			UNIT	SELLING
7		NUMBER	ITEM	STYLE	COST	PRICE
8						
9	Men's wear	66147091	Polo	Salmon Lake	15	34.5
10		68047979	Henleys	Caroga Lake	20	39.5
11		67252066	Tees Short Sleeve Logo	Mount Colden	10	19.5
12		68046404	Fleece	Roaring Brook	20	39.5
13		73012342	Denim Jacket	Bull Point	60	79.5
14		65014099	Sweater	Ridge Trail	20	39.5
15		72024865	Jeans	Kilburn low rise boot	20	39.5
16		71032968	Classic Pants	Woodfalls cargo	25	44.5
17		70033081	Shorts	Bradshaw cargo	20	39.5
18						
19						
20	Women's wear	97170590	Message Tees	Beauty and Brains	6	15.5
21		81367542	Tanks/Camis	Cecilia	5	12.5
22		81373714	Knits	Danielle	15	24.5
23		82050120	Pullover Fleece	Kylie velvet	20	39.5
24		82048637	Track Jackets	Jaime	40	59.5
25		80042350	Sweaters	Alyssa	30	49.5
26		90014006	Denim Jackets	Tori	65	89.5
27		90014048	Outerwear	Heather	75	128
28		86045021	Jeans	Ashley super flare	20	39.5
29		85094002	Active Pants	Jane stitch	15	34.5
30		88033853	Denim Skirts	Cynthia	28	54.5

Source: http://www.abercrombie.com/anf/lifestyles/html/homepage.html

ACTIVITY 8: FBLA CLUB MEMBERS 2

New Skills Reinforced:

In this activity, you will practice how to:

1. retrieve a stored file.
2. save an existing file using a different name.
3. change page orientation to landscape.

Activity Overview:

The following activity illustrates how spreadsheets can be used to list student's names and complete addresses. This activity expands on the FBLA club spreadsheet created in Activity 5.

Instructions:

NEW SKILL 1. Open the file FBLA CLUB MEMBERS previously created in Activity 5.

Note: Unless otherwise stated, the font should be set to Arial, the font size to 10 point.

2. Change the Activity # in row 1 to read Activity 8.
3. Type the data in columns F, G, H and I as shown.
4. Format the width of column F to 24.0 and left align.
5. Format the width of column G to 16.0 and left align.
6. Center columns H and I.
7. In cells A10 and A11, type 1 and 2 respectively as shown.
8. Use the AutoFill feature to complete the series of numbers in the remaining cells. To do this, select cells A10 – A11. While the cells are selected, click the bottom right-hand corner of cell A11 until the mouse pointer changes to a "+" sign. Now drag the mouse pointer down to cell A29 and release the mouse button. The cells should now be filled to complete the number sequence for cells A10 – A29.
9. Bold and underline cells F9 – I9.
10. Carefully proofread your work for accuracy.

NEW SKILL 11. Save the spreadsheet as FBLA CLUB MEMBERS 2.

12. Analyze the changes made to the data in the spreadsheet.
13. Set the Print Area to include all cells containing data in the spreadsheet.

NEW SKILL 14. Print Preview and adjust the Page Setup so that the spreadsheet fits on one page. Set the page orientation to landscape.

15. Print a copy of the spreadsheet if required by your instructor.

ACTIVITY 8: FBLA CLUB MEMBERS 2 DATA SPREADSHEET

	A	B	C	D	E	F	G	H	I
1	Activity 8 Student Name								
2	**ALAMO Heights High School**								
3	6900 Broadway								
4	San Antonio, Texas 78209								
5									
6	**Future Business Leaders of America (FBLA) Club Members 2006-07**								
7	Advisor: Lea Meyers								
8									
9		**LAST**	**FIRST**	**ID #**	**YEAR**	ADDRESS	CITY	STATE	ZIP
10	1	Chan	Zhu Na	1988	Senior	4502 Misty Run	San Antonio	TX	78217
11	2	Chao	Hao Ting	9978	Sophomore	525 Evans Ave	San Antonio	TX	78209
12		Chu	Jason	3680	Freshman	1983 Oakwell Farms Pkwy	San Antonio	TX	78218
13		Chung	Marvin	3229	Junior	102 E Wildwood Drive	San Antonio	TX	78212
14		Forsyth	Amanda	4322	Junior	112 E Pecan Street	San Antonio	TX	78205
15		Frederic	Rashida	1526	Senior	2626 Country Hollow Street	San Antonio	TX	78209
16		Huang	Sze Wai	7957	Senior	105 Harriet Drive	San Antonio	TX	78216
17		Hudson	Daniel	5044	Freshman	438 Honey Blvd	San Antonio	TX	78220
18		Jefferson	Henry	3996	Sophomore	222 Wellesley Blvd	San Antonio	TX	78209
19		Khazanovich	Karina	0155	Freshman	405 Bronzeglo Drive	San Antonio	TX	78239
20		Leung	Jenny	0960	Junior	2827 Chisholm Trail	San Antonio	TX	78217
21		Liang	Shun Yi	3771	Senior	2723 Briarfield Drive	San Antonio	TX	78230
22		Moses	Shani	2289	Sophomore	2555 NE Loop 410	San Antonio	TX	78217
23		Nemenko	Ashley	6125	Senior	7709 Broadway Street	San Antonio	TX	78209
24		Soares	Candace	9745	Freshman	1901 Burnet Street	San Antonio	TX	78202
25		St. Fleur	Fadhylla	9509	Freshman	13615 Stony Forest Drive	San Antonio	TX	78231
26		Tan	Joanna	6894	Junior	261 Harmon Drive	San Antonio	TX	78209
27		Tinaz	Murat	7109	Freshman	121 Cliffside Drive	San Antonio	TX	78231
28		Wong	Miao Xian	4533	Sophomore	11430 Whisper Moss Street	San Antonio	TX	78230
29		Zhou	Xuyang	2278	Sophomore	3206 Cripple Creek Street	San Antonio	TX	78209

Source: http://www.fbla-pbl.org/

ACTIVITY 9: MOVIE RELEASE DATES

New Skills Reinforced:

In this activity, you will practice how to:

1. format cells as dates in a spreadsheet.

Activity Overview:

Comingsoon.net provides movie release dates and reviews so consumers can track information on movies. Besides movie release dates, the site offers features, movie and television news, bulletin boards, trailers and clips, previews, DVD news, box office reports, and more. Information comes directly from the studios. Anytime a title goes from an estimated release date to an exact release date, it is the studio that provides the information. As with any industry, release dates change often.

Many factors determine a movie's video release date including box office performance, time of the year, genre, and target audience. Each studio has its own way of determining video release dates that vary from movie to movie.

The following activity illustrates how spreadsheets can be used to list movie titles, release dates, and leading actors and actresses.

Instructions:

1. Create a NEW spreadsheet.
   Note: Unless otherwise stated, the font should be set to Arial, the font size to 10 point.
2. Type the data as shown.
3. Change the font size of A2 to 16 point.
4. Bold rows 4 and 5.
5. Select cells A7 – A8 and use the AutoFill feature to complete the series of numbers for cells A7 – A30.
6. Format the width of column A to 12.0 and left align.
7. Center align cells A5 – A30.
8. Format the width of column B to 30.0 and left align.
9. Format the width of column C to 12.0 and right align.
10. **NEW SKILL** Format column C as dates showing m/dd/yyyy. Example: "1/6/2006."
11. Format the width of column D to 12.0 and center align.
12. Format the width of columns E and F to 24.0 and left align.
13. Carefully proofread your work for accuracy.
14. Save the spreadsheet as MOVIE RELEASE DATES.
15. Analyze the changes made to the data in the spreadsheet.
16. Set the Print Area to include all cells containing data in the spreadsheet.
17. Print Preview and adjust the Page Setup so that the spreadsheet fits on one page. Set the page orientation to landscape.
18. Print a copy of the spreadsheet if required by your instructor.

ACTIVITY 9: MOVIE RELEASE DATES DATA SPREADSHEET

	A	B	C	D	E	F
1	Activity 9 Student Name					
2	MOVIE RELEASE DATES					
3						
4			RELEASE			
5	NUMBER	MOVIE TITLE	DATE	RATING	LEADING ACTOR	LEADING ACTRESS
6						
7	1	BloodRayne	1/6/06	R	Ben Kingsley	Kristanna Loken
8	2	Glory Road	1/13/06	PG	Josh Lucas	(None)
9		Last Holiday	1/13/06	PG	LL Cool J	Queen Latifah
10		The Libertine	1/13/06	NA	Johnny Depp	Samantha Morton
11		Underworld: Evolution	1/20/06	NA	Scott Speedman	Kate Beckinsale
12		Big Momma's House 2	1/27/06	PG-13	Martin Lawrence	Nia Long
13		Curious George	2/10/06	PG	Will Ferrell	Drew Barrymore
14		Firewall	2/10/06	NA	Harrison Ford	Virginia Madsen
15		Final Destination 3	2/10/06	NA	Ryan Merriman	Mary Elizabeth
16		The Pink Panther	2/10/06	PG	Steve Martin	Beyoncé Knowles
17		Date Movie	2/17/06	NA	Eddie Griffin	Alyson Hannigan
18		Freedomland	2/17/06	R	Samuel L. Jackson	Julianne Moore
19		Alpha Dog	2/24/06	R	Justin Timberlake	Emile Hirsch
20		Dave Chappelle's Block Party	3/3/06	NA	Dave Chappelle	Lauryn Hill
21		Failure to Launch	3/3/06	NA	Matthew McConaughey	Sarah Jessica Parker
22		Basic Instinct 2: Risk Addiction	3/10/06	NA	David Morrissey	Sharon Stone
23		The Shaggy Dog	3/10/06	PG	Tim Allen	Kristin Davis
24		Ask the Dust	3/17/06	R	Colin Farrell	Salma Hayek
25		V For Vendetta	3/17/06	R	Hugo Weaving	Natalie Portman
26		The Inside Man	3/24/06	NA	Denzel Washington	Jodie Foster
27		RV	3/24/06	NA	Robin Williams	Kristin Chenoweth
28		Take the Lead	3/24/06	NA	Antonio Banderas	Jenna Dewan
29		Ice Age 2: The Meltdown	3/31/06	G	Ray Romano	Queen Latifah
30		Lucky Number Slevin	3/31/06	NA	Bruce Willis	Lucy Liu

Source: www.comingsoon.net

ACTIVITY 10: S.A.T. SCORES

New Skills Reinforced:

In this activity, you will practice how to:

1. add numbers in a spreadsheet using a formula.
2. use the AutoFill feature to complete formulas.
3. display formulas in a spreadsheet.

Activity Overview:

The new S.A.T. Reasoning Test was administered for the first time on March 12, 2005. Changes to the test include the addition of third-year college preparatory math, more critical reading, and a new writing section. The College Board made these changes to better reflect what students study in high school. The College Board provides students with accessible, accurate information on the test, the latest research findings, and expert contacts. High school students need to know more about what these changes mean to them.

The following activity illustrates how spreadsheets can be used by school personnel to list students and their respective critical reading, math, and writing S.A.T. scores. These scores will then be added to determine the student's total score.

Instructions:

1. Create a NEW spreadsheet.
   Note: Unless otherwise stated, the font should be set to Arial, the font size to 10 point.
2. Type the data as shown.
3. Bold cells A2 and A6.
4. Bold rows 8 and 9.
5. Underline row 8.
6. Format the width of columns A and B to 20.0 and left align.
7. Format the width of columns C – F to 12.0 and center align.
8. NEW SKILL ▸ In cell F10, type the formula =C10+D10+E10
9. NEW SKILL ▸ There is no need to type the formulas for the remaining cells in column F. Instead, use the AutoFill feature to quickly calculate the totals for the remaining cells. To do this, select cell F10, click the bottom right-hand corner of cell F10 until the mouse pointer changes to a "+" sign. Now drag the mouse pointer down to cell F43 and release the mouse button. Cells F10 – F43 should now contain the correct formulas.
10. Alphabetize the students by their last names. To do this, select cells A10 – F43 and sort in ascending order (A–Z). Use the "LAST" column to Sort by.
11. NEW SKILL ▸ Display formulas in your spreadsheet by using <CTRL> + ` to check for accuracy.
12. Carefully proofread your work for accuracy.
13. Save the spreadsheet as SAT SCORES.
14. Analyze the changes made to the data in the spreadsheet.
15. Set the Print Area to include all cells containing data in the spreadsheet.
16. Print Preview and adjust the Page Setup so that the spreadsheet fits on one page.
17. Print a copy of the spreadsheet if required by your instructor.
    Note: Average, Maximum, and Minimum will be completed in Activity 11.

ACTIVITY 10: S.A.T. SCORES DATA SPREADSHEET

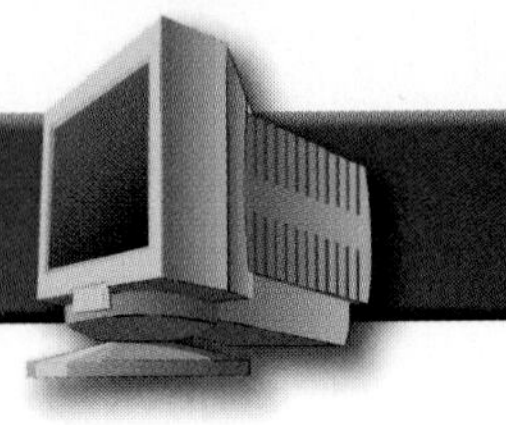

	A	B	C	D	E	F
1	Activity 10 Student Name					
2	John C. Fremont High School					
3	7676 S. San Pedro					
4	Los Angeles, CA 90003					
5						
6	Junior Achievement Scholarship Applicants					
7	Guidance Counselor: Mr. William Seitel					
8			CRITICAL			
9	LAST	FIRST	READING	MATH	WRITING	TOTAL
10	Hom	Lisa	531	578	625	
11	Talignani	Daniel	584	597	632	
12	Bloom	Keith	660	713	702	
13	Doyle	Solomon	565	434	520	
14	Palermo	Andre	483	458	435	
15	Revinskas	Myrna	573	590	573	
16	DiBugnara	Barry	684	621	648	
17	Jimenez	Carlos	698	617	647	
18	Huang	Min Hua	737	771	703	
19	Silva	Pamela	421	505	625	
20	DeAngelis	Eileen	492	531	647	
21	Algoo	John	517	418	563	
22	Jung	Jaymie	681	632	678	
23	Danticat	Burt	712	750	709	
24	Stoppini	Alan	615	576	587	
25	Akaydin	Albert	625	587	471	
26	Merced	Carlos	563	497	487	
27	Zak	Andrew	481	468	432	
28	Savage	Vincent	482	456	472	
29	Kong	Stephanie	685	632	576	
30	Torres	Eddie	686	650	565	
31	Siegfried	Larry	705	712	719	
32	Nemenko	Eric	571	532	545	
33	Personette	Lane	565	485	490	
34	Wong	Jo Jo	717	768	710	
35	Tyshchenko	Russell	618	650	589	
36	Levy	Jarrett	445	598	487	
37	Williams	Romeo	545	571	462	
38	Broth	Marvin	570	526	503	
39	Jean-Pierre	Terry	428	453	412	
40	Orsini	Madelyn	710	621	688	
41	Kvitelman	Morris	481	432	451	
42	Thomas	Raymond	517	475	486	
43	Jones	Michael	557	597	543	
44						
45			CRITICAL			
46			READING	MATH	WRITING	TOTAL
47	AVERAGE					
48	MAXIMUM					
49	MINIMUM					

ACTIVITY 11: S.A.T. SCORES 2

New Skills Reinforced:

In this activity, you will practice how to:

1. use the Average, Maximum, and Minimum functions.
2. sort data in descending order (Z–A).

Activity Overview:

This activity expands on the SAT SCORES spreadsheet created in Activity 10. In this activity, you will compute the average, maximum (highest), and minimum (lowest) critical reading, math, writing, and total S.A.T. scores and then sort the total scores in descending order (highest to lowest).

Instructions:

1. Open the file SAT SCORES previously created in Activity 10.

   Note: Unless otherwise stated, the font should be set to Arial, the font size to 10 point.
2. Change the Activity # in row 1 to read Activity 11.
3. NEW SKILL ▶ Compute the AVERAGE, MAXIMUM, and MINIMUM formulas for column C, CRITICAL READING, as follows:
   a. In cell C47, type =AVERAGE(C10:C43)
   b. In cell C48, type =MAX(C10:C43)
   c. In cell C49, type =MIN(C10:C43)
   d. Select cells C47 – C49 and use the AutoFill feature to copy the formulas to the remaining MATH, WRITING, and TOTAL columns.
4. Format cells C47 – F49 as numbers displaying 0 decimal places.
5. NEW SKILL ▶ Sort the spreadsheet by TOTAL S.A.T. scores (column F) from highest score to lowest score. To do this, select cells A10 – F43 and sort in descending order (Z–A). Use the column "TOTAL" to Sort by. **Note:** The student with the highest TOTAL score will appear on top and the student with the lowest TOTAL score will appear at the bottom.
6. Display formulas in your spreadsheet by using <CTRL> + ` to check for accuracy.
7. Carefully proofread your work for accuracy.
8. Save the spreadsheet as SAT SCORES 2.
9. Analyze the changes made to the data in the spreadsheet.
10. Set the Print Area to include all cells containing data in the spreadsheet.
11. Print Preview and adjust the Page Setup so that the spreadsheet fits on one page.
12. Print a copy of the spreadsheet if required by your instructor.

ACTIVITY 11: S.A.T. SCORES 2 DATA SPREADSHEET

	A	B	C	D	E	F
1	Activity 11 Student Name					
2	**John C. Fremont High School**					
3	7676 S. San Pedro					
4	Los Angeles, CA 90003					
5						
6	**Junior Achievement Scholarship Applicants**					
7	Guidance Counselor: Mr. William Seitel					
8			**CRITICAL**			
9	**LAST**	**FIRST**	**READING**	**MATH**	**WRITING**	**TOTAL**
10	Akaydin	Albert	625	587	471	1683
11	Algoo	John	517	418	563	1498
12	Bloom	Keith	660	713	702	2075
13	Broth	Marvin	570	526	503	1599
14	Danticat	Burt	712	750	709	2171
15	DeAngelis	Eileen	492	531	647	1670
16	DiBugnara	Barry	684	621	648	1953
17	Doyle	Solomon	565	434	520	1519
18	Hom	Lisa	531	578	625	1734
19	Huang	Min Hua	737	771	703	2211
20	Jean-Pierre	Terry	428	453	412	1293
21	Jimenez	Carlos	698	617	647	1962
22	Jones	Michael	557	597	543	1697
23	Jung	Jaymie	681	632	678	1991
24	Kong	Stephanie	685	632	576	1893
25	Kvitelman	Morris	481	432	451	1364
26	Levy	Jarrett	445	598	487	1530
27	Merced	Carlos	563	497	487	1547
28	Nemenko	Eric	571	532	545	1648
29	Orsini	Madelyn	710	621	688	2019
30	Palermo	Andre	483	458	435	1376
31	Personette	Lane	565	485	490	1540
32	Revinskas	Myrna	573	590	573	1736
33	Savage	Vincent	482	456	472	1410
34	Siegfried	Larry	705	712	719	2136
35	Silva	Pamela	421	505	625	1551
36	Stoppini	Alan	615	576	587	1778
37	Talignani	Daniel	584	597	632	1813
38	Thomas	Raymond	517	475	486	1478
39	Torres	Eddie	686	650	565	1901
40	Tyshchenko	Russell	618	650	589	1857
41	Williams	Romeo	545	571	462	1578
42	Wong	Jo Jo	717	768	710	2195
43	Zak	Andrew	481	468	432	1381
44						
45			CRITICAL			
46			READING	MATH	WRITING	TOTAL
47	AVERAGE					
48	MAXIMUM					
49	MINIMUM					

ACTIVITY 12: GAP® PAYROLL REGISTER

New Skills Reinforced:

In this activity, you will practice how to:

1. use formulas to multiply, add, and subtract numbers.
2. use parentheses in formulas.
3. use a formula that references the answer to another cell's formula.
4. change page margins.

Activity Overview:

The Gap® is a retail clothing store located worldwide that offers premium clothing and accessories. Their fresh, casual, and American style of clothing bring consumers a wide assortment to choose from. The Gap® has everything people need to express a personal style. From jeans and T's, to khakis and oxfords, the Gap® has fashion at great prices for adults, teens, kids, and babies.

The following activity illustrates how the Gap® can use spreadsheets to compute payroll amounts for its employees (known as a payroll register).

Instructions:

1. Create a NEW spreadsheet.

   Note: Unless otherwise stated, the font should be set to Arial, the font size to 10 point.
2. Type the data as shown.
3. Bold cells A2 – L11.
4. Underline row 11.
5. Format the width of columns A, B, and C to 12.0 and left align.
6. Format the width of columns D and E to 10.0 and center align.
7. Format the width of columns F – L to 10.0 and right align.
8. Format cells E13 – L32 as numbers displaying 2 decimal places.
9. **NEW SKILL** Compute GROSS PAY, all deductions, and NET PAY for the first employee as follows:
   a. GROSS PAY=HOURS WORKED*HOURLY RATE -> In cell F13, type =D13*E13
   b. FEDERAL TAX=GROSS PAY*15 % -> In cell G13, type =F13*15%
   c. SOCIAL SEC. TAX=GROSS PAY*6.2 % -> In cell H13, type =F13*6.2%
   d. MEDICARE TAX=GROSS PAY*1.45 % -> In cell I13, type =F13*1.45%
   e. STATE TAX=GROSS PAY*4 % -> In cell J13, type =F13*4%
   f. PENSION=GROSS PAY*3 % -> In cell K13, type =F13*3%
   g. NET PAY=GROSS PAY-(the sum of all deductions) -> In cell L13, type =F13-(G13+H13+I13+J13+K13)
10. Use the AutoFill feature to copy the formulas to the remaining cells for each of the employees.
11. Display formulas in your spreadsheet by using <CTRL> + ` to check for accuracy.

12. Carefully proofread your work for accuracy.
13. Save the spreadsheet as GAP PAYROLL REGISTER.
14. Analyze the changes made to the data in the spreadsheet.
15. Set the Print Area to include all cells containing data in the spreadsheet.

NEW SKILL

16. Print Preview and adjust the Page Setup so that the spreadsheet fits on one page. Set the page orientation to landscape. Change the left and right margins to .25 inches.
17. Print a copy of the spreadsheet if required by your instructor.

ACTIVITY 12: GAP® PAYROLL REGIST

				D	E	F	G	H	I	J	K	L
				HOURS WORKED	HOURLY RATE	GROSS PAY	FEDERAL TAX	SOCIAL SEC. TAX	MEDICARE TAX	STATE TAX	PENSION	NET PAY
				35	13.25							
				37	12.25							
15	[illegible]			40	11.50							
16	975587	Estarada	Yana	33	10.50							
17	952779	Grant	Gaston	28	10.25							
18	990736	Jiang	Shun Yi	32	11.75							
19	469051	Karaday	Steffen	36	13.00							
20	633771	Leja	Cynthia	34	11.75							
21	107686	Liao	Xuyang	33	11.50							
22	826556	Lin	Miao Yun	24	10.75							
23	973830	Lucero	Jason	40	12.75							
24	101002	Manakhimov	Ilya	30	11.75							
25	172289	Mandley	Kyle	28	12.25							
26	131161	Milnes	Fatin	32	12.25							
27	918415	Rodriguez	Sylvia	31	12.75							
28	966894	Silvera	Yelena	36	12.00							
29	877827	Sobolewska	Ashley	40	12.50							
30	872336	Vasilyeva	Joanna	34	10.25							
31	525338	Wan	John	26	11.00							
32	429509	Wang	Shirley	35	12.25							

Source: http://www.gap.com

ANDINGS

New Skills Reinforced:

In this activity, you will practice how to:

1. print gridlines in a spreadsheet.
2. copy and paste formulas.

ew:

sport played all over the world and has become one of the most popular winter sports. The League® (NHL®) also televises many games nationally so its fans can watch their favorite teams. eople play and watch hockey worldwide and it has become an obsession to some fans. Many daily e United States and Canada list the NHL® Standings so sports enthusiasts can see how their favorite e doing as compared to other teams in the NHL®.

he following activity illustrates how newspapers use spreadsheets to list the NHL® Standings.

Instructions:

1. Create a NEW spreadsheet.
   Note: Unless otherwise stated, the font should be set to Arial, the font size to 10 point.
2. Type the data as shown.
3. Set the top margin to .50 inches and the bottom margin to .25 inches.
4. Bold cell A2 and change the font size to 20 point.
5. Bold cells C4 and C29 and change the font size to 14 point.
6. Bold cells A5, A13, A21, A30, A38, and A46 and change the font size to 12 point.
7. Bold rows 6, 14, 22, 31, 39 and 47.
8. Format the width of column A to 15.0 and columns B – H to 8.0.
9. Center align cells B6 – H52.
10. Enter the formula for PTS (Points) for the first team, The New Jersey Devils® (NEW JERSEY), as follows:
    PTS=W*2+OTL ***Note:*** *W(Wins), OTL(Overtime Losses)* -> In cell E7, type =B7*2+D7

NEW SKILL

11. To complete the PTS column for each team, copy and paste the formula in cell E7 to cells E8 – E11, E15 – E19, E23 – E27, E32 – E36, E40 – E44, and E48 – E52.
12. Enter the formula for DIFF (Difference in goals scored) for the first team, The New Jersey Devils (NEW JERSEY), as follows:
    DIFF=GF-GA (***Note:*** *GF(Goals For), GA(Goals Against)*) -> In cell H7, type =F7-G7

NEW SKILL

13. To complete the DIFF column for each team, copy and paste the formula in cell H7 to cells H8 – H11, H15 – H19, H23 – H27, H32 – H36, H40 – H44, and H48 – H52.
14. Display formulas in your spreadsheet by using <CTRL> + ` to check for accuracy.
15. Carefully proofread your work for accuracy.
16. Save the spreadsheet as NHL STANDINGS.
17. Analyze the changes made to the data in the spreadsheet.
18. Set the Print Area to include all cells containing data in the spreadsheet.

NEW SKILL

19. Print Preview and adjust the Page Setup so that the spreadsheet fits on one page. Set the page to print gridlines.
20. Print a copy of the spreadsheet if required by your instructor.

ACTIVITY 13: NHL® STANDINGS DATA SPREADSHEET

	A	B	C	D	E	F	G	H
1	Activity 13 Student Name							
2	N.H.L. STANDINGS 2005-06							
3								
4			EASTERN CONFERENCE					
5	ATLANTIC DIVISION							
6		W	L	OTL	PTS	GF	GA	DIFF
7	NEW JERSEY	46	27	9		242	229	
8	PHILADELPHIA	45	26	11		267	259	
9	RANGERS	44	26	12		257	215	
10	ISLANDERS	36	40	6		230	278	
11	PITTSBURGH	22	46	14		244	316	
12								
13	NORTHEAST DIVISION							
14		W	L	OTL	PTS	GF	GA	DIFF
15	OTTAWA	52	21	9		314	211	
16	BUFFALO	52	24	6		281	239	
17	MONTREAL	42	31	9		243	247	
18	TORONTO	41	33	8		257	270	
19	BOSTON	29	37	16		230	266	
20								
21	SOUTHEAST DIVISION							
22		W	L	OTL	PTS	GF	GA	DIFF
23	CAROLINA	52	22	8		294	260	
24	TAMPA BAY	43	33	6		252	260	
25	ATLANTA	41	33	8		281	275	
26	FLORIDA	37	34	11		240	257	
27	WASHINGTON	29	41	12		237	306	
28								
29			WESTERN CONFERENCE					
30	CENTRAL DIVISION							
31		W	L	OTL	PTS	GF	GA	DIFF
32	DETROIT	58	16	8		305	209	
33	NASHVILLE	49	25	8		259	227	
34	COLUMBUS	35	43	4		223	279	
35	CHICAGO	26	43	13		211	285	
36	ST. LOUIS	21	46	15		197	292	
37								
38	NORTHWEST DIVISION							
39		W	L	OTL	PTS	GF	GA	DIFF
40	CALGARY	46	25	11		218	200	
41	COLORADO	43	30	9		283	257	
42	EDMONTON	41	28	13		256	251	
43	VANCOUVER	42	32	8		256	255	
44	MINNESOTA	38	36	8		231	215	
45								
46	PACIFIC DIVISION							
47		W	L	OTL	PTS	GF	GA	DIFF
48	DALLAS	53	23	6		265	218	
49	SAN JOSE	44	27	11		266	242	
50	ANAHEIM	43	27	12		254	229	
51	LOS ANGELES	42	35	5		249	270	
52	PHOENIX	38	39	5		246	271	

Source: www.NHL.com

ACTIVITY 14: CHICAGO WHITE SOX®

New Skills Reinforced:

In this activity, you will practice how to:
1. divide numbers in a formula.
2. increase a cell's decimal places.
3. use the SUM function.

Activity Overview:

Major League Baseball® (MLB®) is the highest level of play in professional baseball in the world. Major League Baseball® refers to the entity that operates North America's two top leagues, the National League® (NL®) and the American League® (AL®). The Major League® season generally runs from early April through the end of October. There are 30 teams in the 2 leagues: 16 in the National League® and 14 in the American League®.

When the regular season ends, eight teams enter the post-season playoffs. In 2005, the Chicago White Sox® were the World Champions. The following activity illustrates how spreadsheets can be used to list and compute baseball statistics.

Instructions:

1. Create a NEW spreadsheet.

   Note: Unless otherwise stated, the font should be set to Arial, the font size to 10 point.
2. Type the data as shown.
3. Format the width of column A to 18.0 and left align.
4. Bold cell A2 and change the font size to 14 point.
5. Bold rows 4, 23, 26, and 41.
6. Underline rows 4 and 26.
7. Center align columns B – K.
8. NEW SKILL Enter the formula for the AVG (Batting Average) for the first player as follows:

   AVG=HITS/AB (***Note:*** *AB (At Bats)* -> In cell F6, type =E6/D6
9. Use the AutoFill feature to copy the Batting Averages (AVG) formula down in column F for the remaining players.
10. NEW SKILL Format cells F6 – F23 as numbers displaying 3 decimal places.
11. Enter the formula for the E.R.A. (Earned Run Average) for the first pitcher as follows:

    E.R.A.=Runs/Innings*9 -> In cell G28, type =F28/E28*9
12. Use the AutoFill feature to copy the Earned Run Averages (E.R.A.) formula down in column G for the remaining pitchers.
13. Format cells G28 – G41 as numbers displaying 2 decimal places.

NEW SKILL

14. Use the SUM function to compute the TOTALS for all columns with the exception of the AVG and E.R.A. columns. *These columns require a different formula (provided in the next step) since you cannot sum averages.*
    a. In cell C23, type =SUM(C6:C22)
    b. Use the AutoFill feature to copy this formula to cells D23 – K23 (***Note:*** *cell F23's formula will be changed in the next step*).
    c. In cell B41, type =SUM(B28:B40)
    d. Use the AutoFill feature to copy this formula to cells C41 – I41 (***Note:*** *cell G41's formula will be changed in the next step*).
15. Compute the totals of the AVG and E.R.A. columns as follows:
    a. Total AVG -> In cell F23, type =E23/D23
    b. Total E.R.A. -> In cell G41, type =F41/E41*9
16. Display formulas in your spreadsheet by using <CTRL> + ` to check for accuracy.
17. Carefully proofread your work for accuracy.
18. Save the spreadsheet as CHICAGO WHITE SOX.
19. Analyze the changes made to the data in the spreadsheet.
20. Set the Print Area to include all cells containing data in the spreadsheet.
21. Print Preview and adjust the Page Setup so that the spreadsheet fits on one page. Set the page orientation to landscape and the page margins to .50 inches.
22. Print a copy of the spreadsheet if required by your instructor.

ACTIVITY 14: CHICAGO WHITE SOX® DATA SPREADSHEET

	A	B	C	D	E	F	G	H	I	J	K
1	Activity 14 Student Name										
2	CHICAGO WHITE SOX WORLD SERIES CHAMPIONS 2005										
3											
4	PLAYER'S NAME	POS	GAMES	AB	HITS	AVG	RUNS	2B	3B	HR	RBI
5											
6	Aaron Rowand	OF	157	578	156		77	30	5	13	69
7	Paul Konerko	1B	158	575	163		98	24	0	40	100
8	Jermaine Dye	OF	145	529	145		74	29	2	31	86
9	Tadahito Iguchi	2B	135	511	142		74	25	6	15	71
10	Scott Podsednick	OF	129	507	147		80	28	1	0	25
11	Carl Everett	DH	135	490	123		58	17	2	23	87
12	Juan Uribe	SS	146	481	121		58	23	3	16	71
13	A.J. Pierzynski	C	128	460	118		61	21	0	18	56
14	Joe Crede	3B	132	432	109		54	21	0	22	62
15	Paul Ozuna	2B	70	203	56		27	7	2	0	11
16	Timo Perez	OF	76	179	39		13	8	0	2	15
17	Chris Widger	C	45	141	34		18	8	0	4	11
18	Willie Harris	2B	56	121	31		17	2	1	1	8
19	Frank Thomas	DH	34	105	23		19	3	0	12	26
20	Geoff Blum	3B	31	95	19		6	2	1	1	3
21	Ross Gload	1B	28	42	7		2	2	0	0	5
22	Brian Anderson	OF	13	34	6		3	1	0	2	3
23	TOTALS										
24											
25											
26		WINS	LOSSES	GAMES	INNINGS	RUNS	E.R.A.	K	SAVES		
27											
28	Mark Buehrle	16	8	33	237	99		149	0		
29	Freddy Garcia	14	8	33	228	102		146	0		
30	Jon Garland	18	10	32	221	93		115	0		
31	Jose Contreras	15	7	32	205	91		154	0		
32	Orlando Hernandez	9	9	24	128	77		91	1		
33	Luis Vizcaino	6	5	65	70	30		43	0		
34	Cliff Politte	7	1	68	67	15		57	1		
35	Brandon McCarthy	3	2	12	67	30		48	0		
36	Neal Cotts	4	0	69	60	15		58	0		
37	Dustin Hermanson	2	4	57	57	17		33	34		
38	Damaso Damarte	3	4	66	45	21		54	4		
39	Bobby Jenks	1	1	32	39	15		50	6		
40	Shingo Takatsu	1	2	31	29	19		32	8		
41	TOTALS										

Source: http://chicago.whitesox.mlb.com/NASApp/mlb/index.jsp?c_id=cws

ACTIVITY 15: BEST BUY®

New Skills R

In this activity, you w

1. format a row's heig

ACTIV

Activity Overview:

Best Buy® Co. is one of North America's specialty retailers of consumer electronics, personal computers, entertainment software, and appliances. They are a company that understands the importance of learning and innovation. From personal shopping assistants and Geek Squad to Magnolia Home Theater, Test Drive, and Best Buy for Business, there's a lot going on at Best Buy®. They are committed to offering a broad selection of products at competitive prices. Online prices and selection generally match those in stores.

The following activity illustrates how spreadsheets can be used to compute the digital cameras sold by Best Buy® and their discounted prices including sales tax.

Instructions:

1. Create a NEW spreadsheet.

   Note: Unless otherwise stated, the font should be set to Arial, the font size to 10 point.
2. Type the data as shown. In cell D4, type your name as the Sales Representative.
3. Format the width of column A to 65.0 and left align.
4. Bold cell A2 and change the font size to 14 point.
5. Bold rows 7 and 8.
6. Format the width of columns B – F to 10.0 and right align.
7. **NEW SKILL** Select rows 10 – 30 and change the row height to 18.0.
8. Compute the formulas for the first camera as follows:
   a. SALE PRICE=LIST PRICE-DISCOUNT -> In cell D10, type =B10-C10
   b. SALES TAX=SALES PRICE*6% -> In cell E10, type =D10*6%
   c. FINAL PRICE=SALES PRICE+SALES TAX -> In cell F10, type =D10+E10
9. Format cells B10 – F30 as numbers displaying 2 decimal places.
10. Use the AutoFill feature to copy the formulas down for the remaining cameras.
11. Display formulas in your spreadsheet by using <CTRL> + ` to check for accuracy.
12. Carefully proofread your work for accuracy.
13. Save the spreadsheet as BEST BUY.
14. Analyze the changes made to the data in the spreadsheet.
15. Set the Print Area to include all cells containing data in the spreadsheet.
16. Print Preview and adjust the Page Setup so that the spreadsheet fits on one page. Set the page orientation to landscape.
17. Print a copy of the spreadsheet if required by your instructor.

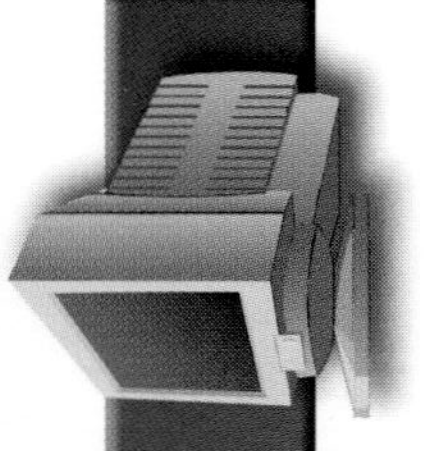

	A	B	C	D	E	F
1	Activity 15 Student Name					
2	BEST BUY		DIGITAL CAMERAS ON SALE 11/12/2005			
3	Morse-Ohio (Store 295)					
4	3840 Morse Road		Sales Rep:	Student's Name		
5	Columbus, OH 43219					
6						
7		LIST		SALE	SALES	FINAL
8	DIGITAL CAMERAS	PRICE	DISCOUNT	PRICE	TAX	PRICE
9						
10	Canon - PowerShot 5.0MP Digital Camera SD400	299.99	15.00			
11	Canon - PowerShot 4.0MP Digital Camera A521	199.00	10.00			
12	Canon - PowerShot 7.1MP Digital Camera SD550	449.99	23.00			
13	Kodak - EasyShare 4.0MP Digital Camera Printer Dock C310 Kit	199.00	10.00			
14	Kodak - EasyShare 5.0MP Zoom Digital Camera with Printer Dock Z740	399.00	20.00			
15	Fuji - FinePix 4.1MP Digital Camera A345	149.00	7.50			
16	Sony - Cyber-shot 7.2MP Digital Camera DSC-W7	349.99	17.50			
17	Sony - Cyber-shot 4.1MP Digital Camera DSC-S60	199.99	10.00			
18	Sony - Cyber-shot 5.1MP Digital Camera - Silver DSC-T5	349.99	17.50			
19	Nikon - Coolpix 5.1MP Digital Camera S1	329.99	16.50			
20	Nikon - Coolpix 5.1MP Digital Camera 5600	249.99	12.50			
21	Kodak - EasyShare 5.0MP Zoom Digital Camera with Dock 2 V550	349.99	0.00			
22	Hewlett-Packard - Photosmart 5.2MP Digital Camera M417	179.99	9.00			
23	Casio - EXILIM 5.0MP Digital Camera - Gray EX-S500GY	349.99	17.50			
24	Sony - Cyber-shot 4.1MP Digital Camera DSC-S40	179.99	9.00			
25	Sony - Cyber-shot 7.2MP Digital Camera - Silver DSC-P200	369.99	19.00			
26	Kodak - EasyShare 5.0MP Digital Camera C340	199.99	10.00			
27	Nikon - Coolpix 4.0MP Digital Camera 4600	179.99	9.00			
28	Olympus - Camedia 5.1MP Digital Camera D-435	149.99	7.50			
29	Fuji - FinePix 5.1MP Digital Camera F460	299.99	15.00			
30	Fuji - FinePix 5.1MP Digital Camera - Black Z1	349.99	17.50			

Source: http://www.bestbuy.com/site/olspage.jsp?id=pcmcat74200050026&type=category

ACTIVITY 16: CIRCUIT CITY®

New Skills Reinforced:

In this activity, you will practice how to:
1. insert a page header.

Activity Overview:

There are a lot of features to consider when consumers are shopping for an MP3 player. Circuit City® Electronics Store will help you through the choices. They offer a wide variety of MP3 players to choose from.

Circuit City's® commitment to customers remains strong. The technologies and solutions they provide can make a consumers shopping experience easier and more enjoyable. Their goal is to ensure just that, whether browsing through one of their stores or surfing the Web site.

The following activity illustrates how spreadsheets can be used to compute Circuit City's® MP3 player discount prices including sales tax.

Instructions:

1. Create a NEW spreadsheet.
   Note: Unless otherwise stated, the font should be set to Arial, the font size to 10 point.
2. Type the data as shown. In cell D4, type your name as the Sales Representative.
3. Bold rows 7 and 8.
4. Format the width of column A to 65.0 and left align.
5. Bold cell A2 and change the font size to 14 point.
6. Format the width of columns B – F to 10.0 and right align.
7. Format cells B10 – F30 as numbers displaying 2 decimal places.
8. Format the height of rows 10 – 30 to 18.0.
9. Compute the formulas as follows for the first MP3 player:
   a. SALE PRICE=LIST PRICE-DISCOUNT -> In cell D10, type =B10-C10
   b. SALES TAX=6%*SALES PRICE -> In cell E10, type =6%*D10
   c. FINAL PRICE=SALE PRICE+SALES TAX -> In cell F10, type =D10+E10
10. Use the AutoFill feature to copy the formulas down for the remaining MP3 players.

NEW SKILL

11. Insert a page header that shows:
    a. Left Section   Activity 16-Student Name
    b. Center Section   CIRCUIT CITY
    c. Right Section   Current Date
12. Display formulas in your spreadsheet by using <CTRL> + ` to check for accuracy.
13. Carefully proofread your work for accuracy.
14. Save the spreadsheet as CIRCUIT CITY.
15. Analyze the changes made to the data in the spreadsheet.
16. Set the Print Area to include all cells containing data in the spreadsheet.
17. Print Preview and adjust the Page Setup so that the spreadsheet fits on one page. Set the page orientation to landscape.
18. Print a copy of the spreadsheet if required by your instructor.

ACTIVITY 16: CIRCUIT CITY® DATA SPREADSHEET

	A	B	C	D	E	F
1						
2	CIRCUIT CITY		MP3 Players & iPods ON SALE 12/09/2005			
3	1045 East Countryline Road					
4	Jackson, MS 39211		Sales Rep:	Your Name		
5						
6						
7		LIST		SALE	SALES	FINAL
8	MP3 PLAYER	PRICE	DISCOUNT	PRICE	TAX	PRICE
9						
10	Toshiba 10GB gigabeat Color Digital Audio Player (MEGF10L)	199.99	25.00			
11	SanDisk 1 GB Digital Audio Player (SDMX31024A18)	104.99	5.00			
12	Creative 1GB Zen Nano Plus (ZNPBU1GB)	119.99	7.50			
13	Samsung 1GB USB Direct-Insert MP3 Player (YPU1Z)	129.99	10.00			
14	iRiver 1GB T10 Jukebox with Color Display (T10BLUE)	149.99	15.00			
15	Sony Network Walkman Digital Music Player (NW-E507)	199.99	40.00			
16	Creative 5GB Zen Micro MP3 Player (ZENMIC5DBLUE)	179.99	20.00			
17	Creative 5GB Zen Micro MP3 Player (ZMIC5RRD)	199.99	20.00			
18	Samsung 1GB Flash Color MP3 Player (YPT8Z)	249.99	50.00			
19	SanDisk Sansa 4GB m260 Digital Audio Player (SDMX34096A18)	199.99	20.00			
20	Olympus microbe 500i Digital Camera/MP3 Player (210010)	249.99	60.00			
21	Toshiba Silver 20GB Digital Audio Player with Color Display (MEGF20S)	249.99	25.00			
22	Apple 2GB Black iPod Nano with Color LCD (MA099LLA)	199.99	10.00			
23	Creative Labs 6GB Zen Micro MP3 Player (ZMIC6BLK)	199.99	15.00			
24	Samsung Micro HDD Jukebox with Color Display (YH-820MC)	229.99	20.00			
25	iRiver H10 5GB MP3 Player Lounge Gray (H10SLATEGREY)	249.99	20.00			
26	Creative Labs Zen Sleek 20GB MP3 Player (ZSEFBKSV)	249.99	15.00			
27	Toshiba 20GB Digital Audio Player with Color Display (MEGF20K)	249.99	25.00			
28	Apple 4GB White iPod Nano with Color LCD (MA005LLA)	249.99	0.00			
29	Creative Labs Zen MicroPhoto 8GB MP3 Player (ZMP8GBGY)	249.99	20.00			
30	iRiver 20GB Jukebox with Color LCD (H10TRANCERED)	299.99	20.00			

Source: http://www.circuitcity.com

ACTIVITY 17: CELEBRITY SEARCHES

New Skills Reinforced:

In this activity, you will practice how to:
1. merge cells in a spreadsheet.
2. insert a page footer.

Activity Overview:

Most people are quite familiar with Internet search engines. Yahoo!®, one of the most popular search engines on the Web, allows users to find content within a specific criteria. Each year, Yahoo!® publishes the top searches its users made in many categories. Looking back at these lists can give anyone a sense of what was popular and in the news for the given year. Since the lists cover everything from celebrities and news to sports and entertainment, a fact seeker or trivia buff will never be without accurate data on what Internet users were looking for.

The following activity illustrates how spreadsheets can be used to list the top celebrity Internet searches made by Yahoo!® users.

Instructions:

1. Create a NEW spreadsheet.

   Note: Unless otherwise stated, the font should be set to Arial, the font size to 10 point.
2. Type the data as shown.
3. Use AutoFill to complete the number sequence in column A.
4. Format the width of column A to 6.0 and center align.
5. Format the width of column B to 28.0 and left align.
6. Format the width of columns C and D to 14.0 and right align.
7. NEW SKILL ▸ Merge and center the text that is shown in cells B1 and B2 across columns B, C, and D.
8. Insert a header that shows:
   a. Left Section Activity 17-Student Name
   b. Center Section CELEBRITY SEARCHES
   c. Right Section Current Date
9. NEW SKILL ▸ Insert a footer that shows:
   a. Center Section PAGE number
10. Carefully proofread your work for accuracy.
11. Save the spreadsheet as CELEBRITY SEARCHES.
12. Analyze the changes made to the data in the spreadsheet.
13. Set the Print Area to include all cells containing data in the spreadsheet.
14. Print Preview and adjust the Page Setup so that the spreadsheet fits on one page.
15. Print a copy of the spreadsheet if required by your instructor.

ACTIVITY 17: CELEBRITY SEARCHES DATA SPREADSHEET

	A	B	C	D
1		Celebrity Top Yahoo! Searches		
2		2005		
3				
4		Overall	Female	Male
5	1	Britney Spears	Britney Spears	50 Cent
6	2	50 Cent	Mariah Carey	Eminem
7		Mariah Carey	Jessica Simpson	Usher
8		Jessica Simpson	Paris Hilton	Nelly
9		Paris Hilton	Ciara	R. Kelly
10		Eminem	Lindsay Lohan	Bow Wow
11		Ciara	Jennifer Lopez	Michael Jackson
12		Lindsay Lohan	Kelly Clarkson	Howard Stern
13		Jennifer Lopez	Hilary Duff	The Game
14		Kelly Clarkson	Shakira	Mike Jones

Source: http://tools.search.yahoo.com/top2005/

ACTIVITY 18: FAST FOOD NUTRITION

New Skills Reinforced:

In this activity, you will practice how to:

1. format text direction.

Activity Overview:

These days, you can't open the newspaper or watch the evening news without being reminded of how out of control America's obesity problem has become. One section of our country's food source that has come under tremendous attack is the fast food industry. Fast food giants, such as McDonalds®, have been criticized for making Americans fat. Lawsuits have even been filed suggesting that if it wasn't for the amazing marketing done by fast food restaurants, our children would be healthier and more physically fit. To combat these attacks, fast food corporations have made nutrition information on their products more readily available. Consumers now have an easier time informing themselves about what they are actually digesting when they indulge in fast food.

The following activity illustrates how spreadsheets can be used to list the nutritional content of popular McDonalds® fast food items.

Instructions:

1. Create a NEW spreadsheet.
   Note: Unless otherwise stated, the font should be set to Arial, the font size to 10 point.
2. Type the data as shown.
3. Bold row 3.
4. Bold cell A1 and change the font size to 20 point.
5. Format the width of column A to 34.0 and left align.
6. Format the width of columns B – M to 13.0 and as numbers displaying 0 decimal places.
7. **NEW SKILL** Format the headings in columns B – M so the text orientation is set to 45 degress.
8. Select cells A4 – M17 and sort them alphabetically in ascending order by the "Menu Item" column.
9. Insert a header that shows:
   a. Left Section — Activity 18-Student Name
   b. Center Section — FAST FOOD NUTRITION
   c. Right Section — Current Date
10. Insert a footer that shows
    a. Center Section — PAGE number
11. Carefully proofread your work for accuracy.
12. Save the spreadsheet as FAST FOOD NUTRITION.
13. Analyze the changes made to the data in the spreadsheet.
14. Set the Print Area to include all cells containing data in the spreadsheet.
15. Print Preview and adjust the Page Setup so that the spreadsheet fits on one page. Set the page orientation to landscape.
16. Print a copy of the spreadsheet if required by your instructor.

ACTIVITY 18: FAST FOOD NUTRITION DATA SPREADSHEET

	A	B	C	D	E	F	G	H	I	J	K	L	M
1	McDonald's Nutrition Information												
2													
3	Menu Item	calories	calories from fat	total fat (g)	% daily value	sat fat (g)	trans fat (g)	cholesterol	sodium	carbs	fiber	sugar	protein
4	hamburger	260	80	9	14	3.5	0.5	30	530	33	1	7	13
5	cheeseburger	310	110	12	19	6	1	40	740	35	1	7	15
6	quarter pounder	420	160	18	27	7	1	70	730	40	3	8	24
7	big mac	560	270	30	47	10	1.5	80	1010	47	3	8	25
8	mcchicken	370	140	16	24	3.5	1	50	810	41	1	5	15
9	small french fries	250	120	13	20	2.5	3.5	0	140	30	3	0	2
10	large french fries	570	270	30	47	6	8	0	330	70	7	0	6
11	chicken nuggets 10 piece	420	220	24	37	5	2.5	60	1120	26	0	0	25
12	caesar salad with grilled chicken	220	60	6	10	3	0	75	890	12	3	13	5
13	newmans own creamy caesar dressing	190	170	18	28	3.5	0	20	500	4	0	2	2
14	egg mcmuffin	300	110	12	18	4.5	0	230	860	30	2	2	17
15	hash browns	140	70	8	13	1.5	2	0	290	15	2	0	1
16	hot fudge sundae	330	80	9	14	6	0	25	170	55	1	48	8
17	baked apple pie	250	100	11	18	3	15	0	150	34	2	13	2

Source: http://www.mcdonalds.com

ACTIVITY 19: CONCERTS

New Skills Reinforced:

In this activity, you will practice how to:
1. change column widths using AutoFit.
2. format cells as currency.

Activity Overview:

Any regular concert attendee knows that the place to buy tickets is Ticketmaster®. Ticketmaster.com® is hands-down the leading e-commerce site distributing tickets for theaters, stadiums, arenas, and clubs all around the country. The company offers many interesting conveniences for their customers. With everything from TicketFast®, an email ticket delivery system, to Ticketmaster® auctions, Ticketmaster® provides easy and secure access to millions of tickets each year.

The following activity illustrates how spreadsheets can be used to list the hottest concerts along with their venue, location, date, and ticket price.

Instructions:

1. Create a NEW spreadsheet.
   Note: Unless otherwise stated, the font should be set to Arial, the font size to 10 point.
2. Type the data as shown.
3. Bold cell A1 and change the font size to 16 point.
4. Bold, underline, and center align row 3.
5. NEW SKILL Format columns A – F to AutoFit so that when the data entered is changed, the column width will automatically adjust.
6. Format column D as dates showing the day and month spelled out. Example: "Sunday, June 4, 2006."
7. Format column E as time showing HH:MM PM.
8. NEW SKILL Format column F as currency displaying 2 decimals and the $ symbol.
9. Insert a header that shows:
   a. Left Section — Activity 19-Student Name
   b. Center Section — CONCERTS
   c. Right Section — Current Date
10. Insert a footer that shows:
    a. Center Section — PAGE number
11. Carefully proofread your work for accuracy.
12. Save the spreadsheet as CONCERTS.
13. Analyze the changes made to the data in the spreadsheet.
14. Set the Print Area to include all cells containing data in the spreadsheet.
15. Print Preview and adjust the Page Setup so that the spreadsheet fits on one page. Set the page orientation to landscape.
16. Print a copy of the spreadsheet if required by your instructor.

ACTIVITY 19: CONCERTS DATA SPREADSHEET

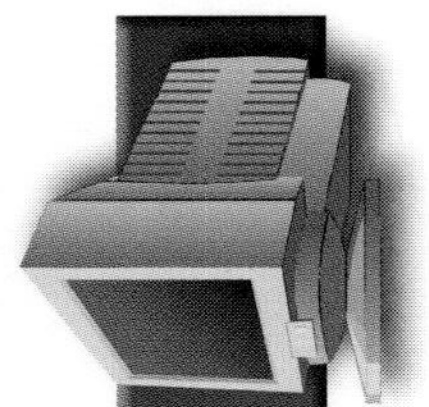

	A	B	C	D	E	F	G
1	Hot Tickets from Ticketmaster.com						
2							
3	Event	Venue	Location	Date	Time	Highest Priced Ticket	
4	Jimmy Buffett and the Coral Reefer Band	Mohegan Sun Arena	Uncasville, CT	6/29/2006	7:00 PM	251	
5	Fall Out Boy	Giant Center	Hershey, PA	5/1/2006	6:30 PM	29.5	
6	Madonna	Madison Square Garden	New York, NY	6/28/2006	8:00 PM	354.5	
7	Pearl Jam	MGM Grand Hotel	Las Vegas, NV	7/6/2006	8:00 PM	51	
8	Kenny Chesney	Van Andel Arena	Grand Rapids, MI	6/2/2006	7:30 PM	64.5	
9	Wicked - a New Musical	Ford Center for the Performing Arts	Chicago, IL	6/9/2006	8:00 PM	122.5	
10	Soul2Soul II with Tim McGraw and Faith Hill	Rupp Arena	Lexington, KY	5/14/2006	7:30 PM	84.5	
11	Monster Jam Monster Truck Racing	Alltel Stadium	Jacksonville, FL	2/24/2007	7:30 PM	25	
12	Dew Action Sports Tour	Pepsi Center	Denver, CO	7/14/2006	3:00 PM	15	

Source: www.ticketmaster.com

ACTIVITY 20: REALITY TV

New Skills Reinforced:

In this activity, you will practice how to:

1. use text wrap within cells.

Activity Overview:

Reality TV has become one of the most popular TV show genres of all time. This surprises many people since television is historically known for allowing actors and actresses to portray characters and tell stories. Reality TV takes the acting out of the mix and features everyday people in a variety of situations. Shows can be competitive, such as Survivor®, shocking, such as Fear Factor®, or even informative, such as MythBusters®. In any case, the stars of the show are not trained actors, and the story they tell is not scripted. Critics will claim that many so-called reality shows are not real at all and blame crafty editing on the many dramas these shows seem to elicit. In any case, viewers are watching, and it doesn't look like these shows will stop any time soon.

The following activity illustrates how spreadsheets can be used to list the most popular reality TV shows.

Instructions:

1. Create a NEW spreadsheet.

   Note: Unless otherwise stated, the font should be set to Arial, the font size to 10 point.
2. Type the data as shown.
3. Change the font size of cell A1 to 16 point.
4. Format the height of row 3 to 30.0 and bold the row.
5. Format the width of column A to 40.0 and left align.
6. Format the width of column B to 13.0 and center align.
7. Format the width of column C to 11.0 and center align.
8. **NEW SKILL** ▸ Format column C to wrap the text within each cell.
9. Format the height of rows 4 – 20 to 40.0.
10. Insert a header that shows:
    a. Left Section Activity 20-Student Name
    b. Center Section REALITY TV
    c. Right Section Current Date
11. Insert a footer that shows
    a. Center Section PAGE number
12. Carefully proofread your work for accuracy.
13. Save the spreadsheet as REALITY TV.
14. Analyze the changes made to the data in the spreadsheet.
15. Set the Print Area to include all cells containing data in the spreadsheet.
16. Print Preview and adjust the Page Setup so that the spreadsheet fits on one page.
17. Print a copy of the spreadsheet if required by your instructor.

ACTIVITY 20: REALITY TV DATA SPREADSHEET

	A	B	C	D	E
1	Most Popular Reality TV Shows				
2					
3	Show	Year Start/End	Airs		
4	American Idol	2002	FOX on Tuesdays at 8 pm		
5	America's Next Top Model	2003	UPN on Wednesdays at 8 pm		
6	The Amazing Race	2001	CBS on Wednesdays at 8 pm		
7	Laguna Beach	2004	MTV on Tuesdays at 10:30 pm		
8	Nashville Star	2003	USA on Tuesdays at 10 pm		
9	The Apprentice	2004	NBC on Mondays at 9 pm		
10	MythBusters	2003	DISC on Wednesdays at 9 pm		
11	Big Brother	2001	CBS on Tuesdays at 9 pm		
12	Pimp My Ride	2004	MTV on Sundays at 9 pm		
13	Survivor	2000	CBS on Thursdays at 8 pm		
14	Miami Ink	2005	TLC on Tuesdays at 10 pm		
15	Beauty and the Geek	2005	WB on Thursdays at 9 pm		
16	Punk'd	2003	MTV on Mondays at 10 pm		
17	My Super Sweet 16	2005	MTV on Tuesdays at 10:30 pm		
18	8th and Ocean	2006	MTV on Tuesdays at 10:30 pm		
19	Viva la Bam	2003/2005	MTV on Sundays at 9:30 pm		
20	Fear Factor	2001	NBC on Tuesdays at 8 pm		

Source: http://www.tv.com/reality/genre/9/summary.html

ACTIVITY 21: CANDY HOLIDAYS

New Skills Reinforced:

In this activity, you will practice how to:

1. insert a clipart image in a spreadsheet.

Activity Overview:

Everyone loves finding out fun facts about fun things. What's better than knowing a cool piece of information about some of the best sweet treats around? The National Confectioners Association has helped to build public awareness of different kinds of candy through national special observances. These dates, which are approved by the United States Senate, get people excited about candy products and give everyone another reason to indulge in their favorite snack. The National Confectioners Association's Web site has a complete list of candy-related holidays along with the history of different candies, recipes, and ways to create family traditions involving candy.

The following activity illustrates how spreadsheets can be used to organize candy holidays. In this activity, you will be inserting a clipart image to enhance the appearance of the spreadsheet.

Instructions:

1. Create a NEW spreadsheet.
   Note: Unless otherwise stated, the font should be set to Arial, the font size to 10 point.
2. Type the data as shown.
3. Bold cell A1 and change the font size to 16 point.
4. Format column B as dates showing DD-Month. Example: "1/3" should appear as "3-Jan."
5. Format the height of row 2 to 60.0.
6. **NEW SKILL** Insert a clipart image depicting candy into the spreadsheet. Place the clipart image next to the title "Candy Holidays" in cell A1. Be sure the image does not cover any text. Resize the clipart image so it is in proportion with the spreadsheet data.
7. Format the width of column A to 43.0 and left align.
8. Bold and underline row 3.
9. Insert a header that shows:
   a. Left Section Activity 21-Student Name
   b. Center Section CANDY HOLIDAYS
   c. Right Section Current Date
10. Insert a footer that shows:
    a. Center Section PAGE number
11. Carefully proofread your work for accuracy.
12. Save the spreadsheet as CANDY HOLIDAYS.
13. Analyze the changes made to the data in the spreadsheet.
14. Set the Print Area to include all cells containing data in the spreadsheet.
15. Print Preview and adjust the Page Setup so that the spreadsheet fits on one page.
16. Print a copy of the spreadsheet if required by your instructor.

ACTIVITY 21: CANDY HOLIDAYS DATA SPREADSHEET

	A	B
1	Candy Holidays	
2		
3	Holiday Titles	Date
4	National Chocolate Covered Cherry Day	1/3
5	National English Toffee Day	1/8
6	National Peanut Brittle Day	1/26
7	National Gum Drop Day	2/15
8	Chocolate Mint Day	2/19
9	National Chocolate Caramel Day	3/19
10	National Chocolate Covered Raisin Day	3/24
11	National Licorice Day	4/12
12	National Chocolate Covered Cashews Day	4/21
13	National Jelly Bean Day	4/22
14	National Nutty Fudge Day	5/12
15	National Chocolate Chip Day	5/15
16	National Taffy Day	5/23
17	Fudge Day	6/16
18	Chocolate Day	7/7
19	Gummi Worm Day	7/15
20	National Lollipop Day	7/20
21	National Milk Chocolate Day	7/28
22	National Chocolate Chip Day	8/4
23	S'more's Day	8/10
24	National Toasted Marshmallow Day	8/30
25	International Chocolate Day	9/13
26	National White Chocolate Day	9/22
27	National Chocolate Day	10/28
28	National Candy Corn Day	10/30
29	National Caramel Apple Day	10/31
30	National Bittersweet Chocolate with Almonds Day	11/7
31	National Cotton Candy Day	12/7
32	National Chocolate Covered Anything Day	12/16
33	National Candy Cane Day	12/26

Source: http://www.candyusa.org/default.asp

ACTIVITY 22: ASTROLOGY

New Skills Reinforced:

In this activity, you will practice how to:
1. insert comments for cells.

Activity Overview:

Astrology is a system of beliefs that some people believe guide personalities and aid in decision-making in one's life. The practice of astrology dates back to the first century BC. Astrology's popularity in today's culture is still very strong. Astrologers try to equate a daily horoscope with what might be going on in the lives of people.

The following activity illustrates how spreadsheets can be used to list astrological personality traits. In this activity, you will add comments to individual cells. Comments are hidden notes that an author of a spreadsheet can use to provide more information about the data of a cell. In this activity, you will be adding comments that provide the birth dates for each astrological sign.

Instructions:

1. Create a NEW spreadsheet.
   Note: Unless otherwise stated, the font should be set to Arial, the font size to 10 point.
2. Type the data as shown.
3. Format the width of column A to 25.0.
4. Use AutoFit to adjust the width of columns B – F.
5. **NEW SKILL** Insert the birthdates shown in Table 1-22 as comments for each corresponding astrology sign shown in column A. For example, Aries should have a comment that reads "3/21 – 4/19."
6. Bold cell A1 and change the font size to 16 point.
7. Bold and center align row 3.
8. Right align cells B4 – F15.
9. Insert a header that shows:
   a. Left Section Activity 22-Student Name
   b. Center Section ASTROLOGY
   c. Right Section Current Date
10. Insert a footer that shows:
    a. Center Section PAGE number
11. Carefully proofread your work for accuracy.
12. Save the spreadsheet as ASTROLOGY.
13. Analyze the changes made to the data in the spreadsheet.
14. Set the Print Area to include all cells containing data in the spreadsheet.
15. Print Preview and adjust the Page Setup so that the spreadsheet fits on one page. Set the page orientation to landscape and to show comments at the end of the sheet.
16. Print a copy of the spreadsheet if required by your instructor.

ACTIVITY 22: ASTROLOGY DATA SPREADSHEET

	A	B	C	D	E	F
1	Personality Traits for Astrological Signs					
2						
3	Sign	Characteristic 1	Characteristic 2	Characteristic 3	Characteristic 4	Characteristic 5
4	Aries	Spiritual Warrior	Initiator	Pioneer	Daredevil	Survivor
5	Taurus	Beauty	Inner Peace	Deprivation	Denial	Abundance
6	Gemini	Adaptable Intellect	Indecisive	Witty	Eloquent	Networker
7	Cancer	Sensitive	Moody	Protective	Nurturing	Sympathetic
8	Leo	Heart	Centerstage	Courage	Actor	Ambitious
9	Virgo	Fixed	Meticulous	Perfectionist	Analytical	Systematic
10	Libra	Idealist	Sociable	Pleaser	Dependent	Self-Indulgent
11	Scorpio	Healer	Psychic	Alchemist	Control	Fear
12	Sagittarius	Inspiration	Vast	Scattered	Traveler	Explorer
13	Capricorn	Master Manifester	Business Whiz	Efficient	Practical	Responsible
14	Aquarius	Scientist	Innovator	Likes to Experiment	Genius	Original
15	Pisces	Empathic	Sensitive	Oneness	Separation Issues	Imaginative

Source: http://www.circlesoflight.com/astrology-articles/astrology-overview-1.shtml

Table 1-22

Add the birthdates provided below as comments to each corresponding astrology sign's cell in column A.

Sign	Birth Dates
Aries	3/21 - 4/19
Taurus	4/20 - 5/20
Gemini	5/21 - 6/21
Cancer	6/22 - 7/22
Leo	7/23 - 8/22
Virgo	8/23 - 9/22
Libra	9/23 - 10/22
Scorpio	10/23 - 11/22
Sagittarius	11/23 - 12/21
Capricorn	12/22 - 1/19
Aquarius	1/20 - 2/18
Pisces	2/19 - 3/20

ACTIVITY 23: XBOX 360®

New Skills Reinforced:

In this activity, you will practice how to:

1. format cells to currency using the dollar sign button on the formatting toolbar.

Activity Overview:

Xbox 360® sets a new pace for digital entertainment. More than just a cutting-edge game system, Xbox 360® integrates high-definition video, DVD movie playback, digital music, photos, and online connectivity into one sleek, small tower.

The following activity illustrates how spreadsheets can be used to compute a sales representative's commission on Xbox 360® games.

Instructions:

1. Create a NEW spreadsheet.
   Note: Unless otherwise stated, the font should be set to Arial, the font size to 10 point.
2. Type the data as shown.
3. Format the width of column A to 50.0 and left align.
4. Format the width of column B to 8.0 and right align
5. **NEW SKILL** Select cells B9 – B33 and format them as currency style by clicking on the "$" button on the formatting toolbar.
6. Format the width of column C to 10.0 and center align.
7. Bold cell A2 and change the font size to 16 point.
8. Compute the formulas for the TOTAL SALES and COMMISSION for the first Game/Accessory as follows:
   a. TOTAL SALES=UNIT PRICE*UNITS SOLD -> In cell D9, type =B9*C9
   b. COMMISSION=5%*TOTAL SALES -> In cell E9, type =5%*D9
9. Use the AutoFill feature to copy the formulas down in the TOTAL SALES and COMMISSION columns.
10. Enter formulas to total columns D and E.
11. Format the width of columns D and E to 13.0 and right align.
12. **NEW SKILL** Select cells D9 – E35 and format them as currency style by clicking on the "$" button on the formatting toolbar.
13. Bold rows 3 – 7 and 35.
14. Display formulas in your spreadsheet by using <CTRL> + ` to check for accuracy.
15. Carefully proofread your work for accuracy.
16. Save the spreadsheet as XBOX 360.
17. Analyze the changes made to the data in the spreadsheet.
18. Set the Print Area to include all cells containing data in the spreadsheet.
19. Print Preview and adjust the Page Setup so that the spreadsheet fits on one page.
20. Print a copy of the spreadsheet if required by your instructor.

ACTIVITY 23: XBOX 360® DATA SPREADSHEET

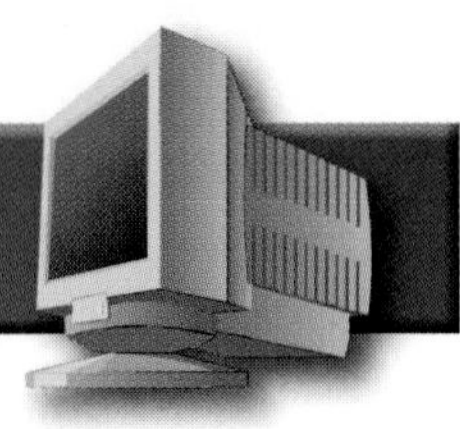

	A	B	C	D	E
1	Activity 23 Student Name				
2	Xbox 360 Games & Accessories				
3	STUDENT'S NAME				
4	MONTHLY COMMISSION REPORT				
5					
6		UNIT	UNITS	TOTAL	
7	GAME/ACCESSORY	PRICE	SOLD	SALES	COMMISSION
8					
9	Amped 3	59.99	22		
10	Call of Duty 2	59.99	34		
11	Condemned: Criminal Origins	59.99	28		
12	Dead or Alive 4	59.99	37		
13	FIFA 2006	59.99	26		
14	Full Auto	59.99	28		
15	Kameo: Elements of Power	49.99	22		
16	Madden NFL 2006	59.99	54		
17	NBA 2K6	59.99	46		
18	NBA Live 2006	59.99	48		
19	Need for Speed: Most Wanted	59.99	37		
20	NHL 2K6	59.99	29		
21	Perfect Dark Zero Limited Collector's Edition	59.99	35		
22	Project Gotham Racing 3	49.99	39		
23	Quake 4	59.99	27		
24	Ridge Racer 6	59.99	23		
25	The Godfather	59.99	25		
26	Tiger Woods PGA Tour 2006	59.99	36		
27	Tony Hawk's American Wasteland	59.99	50		
28	Top Spin 2	59.99	26		
29	True Crimes: New York City	59.99	44		
30	Xbox 360 Peter Jackson's King Kong	59.99	30		
31	Wireless Network Adapter	99.99	16		
32	Wireless Controller	69.99	18		
33	Play and Charge Kit	19.99	10		
34					
35	TOTALS				

Source: http://www.toysrus.com

ACTIVITY 24: MUSIC STORE CHECKBOOK

New Skills Reinforced:

In this activity, you will practice how to:

1. use the AutoSum button on the standard toolbar.

Activity Overview:

Virgin Records™ began in the early 1970s as a small, independent label based in London. Today, Virgin Records™ is part of EMI, the third largest music company in the world. A wide array of artists call Virgin their recording home.

Every successful business must have an accurate accounting system. Businesses must also safeguard cash and cash activities. Businesses usually make daily deposits and pay all their bills by check. These methods help maintain internal control and are an excellent system for protecting their assets.

The following activity illustrates how spreadsheets can be used to update a checkbook register by listing dates with their respective deposits and checks.

Instructions:

1. Create a NEW spreadsheet.
   Note: Unless otherwise stated, the font should be set to Arial, the font size to 10 point.
2. Type the data as shown.
3. Format the width of column A to 12.0 and left align
4. Format cells A10 – A40 as dates showing m/dd/yyyy.
5. Format the width of column B to 12.0 and center align.
6. Format the width of column C to 12.0 and right align.
7. Format cells C10 – C43 as numbers displaying 2 decimal places.
8. Format the width of column D to 20.0.
9. Format the width of column E to 12.0 and center align.
10. Format the width of columns F and G to14.0 and right align.
11. Format cells F10 – G43 as numbers displaying 2 decimal places.
12. Bold cell A2 and change the font size to 16 point.
13. Bold rows 3 – 9 and row 43.
14. Underline row 9.
15. In cell G10, type 35431 for the "Balance brought forward."
16. Enter a formula to calculate the BALANCE for the first transaction in the check register as follows:
    BALANCE=BALANCE+DEPOSITS-WITHDRAWALS -> In cell G11, type =G10+C11-F11
17. Use the AutoFill feature to copy the BALANCE formula down for the remaining transactions shown in column G.
18. **NEW SKILL** Position the cursor in cell C43 and click on the "AutoSum" button on the standard toolbar to sum cells C11 – C40. Repeat this procedure in cell F43 to sum cells F11 – F41.
19. Display formulas in your spreadsheet by using <CTRL> + ` to check for accuracy.
20. Carefully proofread your work for accuracy.
21. Save the spreadsheet as MUSIC STORE CHECKBOOK.
22. Analyze the changes made to the data in the spreadsheet.
23. Set the Print Area to include all cells containing data in the spreadsheet.
24. Print Preview and adjust the Page Setup so that the spreadsheet fits on one page.
25. Print a copy of the spreadsheet if required by your instructor.

ACTIVITY 24: MUSIC STORE CHECKBOOK DATA SPREADSHEET

	A	B	C	D	E	F	G
1	Activity 24 Student Name						
2	VIRGIN RECORDS						
3	150 Fifth Avenue						
4	New York, NY 10011						
5							
6							
7	CHECKBOOK REGISTER						
8							
9	DATE	DEPOSIT#	DEPOSITS		CHECK#	WITHDRAWALS	BALANCE
10	1/7/06			Balance brought forward			
11	1/8/06	543	785.23				
12					932	123.65	
13	1/9/06	544	1,245.32				
14					933	354.23	
15					934	789.23	
16					935	1456.87	
17					936	3156.32	
18					937	547.36	
19	1/10/06	545	4,587.00				
20					938	654.32	
21					939	698.34	
22	1/11/06	546	2,354.87				
23					940	789.32	
24					941	654.78	
25					942	3691.54	
26					943	547.32	
27	1/12/06	547	3,654.45				
28					944	789.23	
29					945	785.23	
30	1/13/06	548	3,254.56				
31					946	741.32	
32							
33	1/14/06	549	2,365.87				
34					947	783.21	
35					948	782.32	
36	1/15/06	550	6,874.56				
37					949	5472.78	
38					950	785.64	
39					951	478.32	
40	1/16/06	551	3,291.65				
41					952	789.38	
42							
43	TOTALS						

ACTIVITY 25: SALES REPORT

New Skills Reinforced:

None. This activity provides additional reinforcement in using many of the skills introduced in previous activities.

Activity Overview:

Sales are the lifeline of all businesses. Without sales, a business could not survive. A business's sales force must be motivated to sell the company's products or services. To accomplish this, businesses usually offer their sales staff a compensation program to help increase sales which leads to increased profits.

Incentive programs consist of commissions, bonus plans, merchandise, prizes, profit sharing, or other rewards that are offered to salespeople to compel them to sell more. However, most businesses use some form of cash commission incentive to motivate their sales staff.

The following activity illustrates how a spreadsheet can be used to compute the commissions earned by Wireless Connections' sales force and add the commissions to their base salary.

Instructions:

1. Create a NEW spreadsheet.
   Note: Unless otherwise stated, the font should be set to Arial, the font size to 10 point.
2. Format row 9 to wrap the text within each cell.
3. Type the data as shown.
4. Format the width of column A to 10.0 and left align.
5. Format the width of columns B and C to 14.0 and left align.
6. Format the width of columns D – G to 13.0 and right align.
7. Format cells D11 – G45 as numbers displaying 2 decimal places.
8. Bold cell A2 and change the font size to 16 point.
9. Bold rows 7 – 9.
10. Compute the formulas for the first employee as follows:
    a. COMMISSION=5%*SALES -> In cell F11, type =5%*E11
    b. TOTAL SALARY=BASE SALARY+COMMISSION -> In cell G11, type =D11+F11
11. Use the AutoFill feature to copy the formulas down for the COMMISSION and TOTAL SALARY columns for the remaining employees.
12. Enter formulas to calculate the Totals, Average, Maximum, and Minimum for columns D – G.
13. Bold rows 42 – 45.
14. Display formulas in your spreadsheet by using <CTRL> + ` to check for accuracy.
15. Carefully proofread your work for accuracy.
16. Save the spreadsheet as SALES REPORT.
17. Analyze the changes made to the data in the spreadsheet.
18. Set the Print Area to include all cells containing data in the spreadsheet.
19. Print Preview and adjust the Page Setup so that the spreadsheet fits on one page.
20. Print a copy of the spreadsheet if required by your instructor.

ACTIVITY 25: SALES REPORT DATA SPREADSHEET

	A	B	C	D	E	F	G
1	Activity 25 Student Name						
2	WIRELESS CONNECTIONS						
3	1022 Monaco Parkway						
4	Denver, CO 80220						
5							
6							
7	January 2006 Sales Report						
8							
9	EMPLOYEE NUMBER	LAST	FIRST	BASE SALARY	SALES	5% COMMISSION	TOTAL SALARY
10							
11	24871	Agyemang	Rashida	500	14569		
12	60155	Asani	Valdete	1000	12057		
13	18835	Amramov	Sharon	1500	15987		
14	56291	Anthony	Brianna	700	8965		
15	91526	Bhuiyan	Julie	800	4569		
16	31994	Campbell	Shani	900	8796		
17	92211	Charles	Anna	1000	11236		
18	65815	Colon	Vanessa	600	21543		
19	31825	Depusoir	Melissa	700	14567		
20	31988	Diga	Shantell	500	17896		
21	69978	Jarara	Amir	1200	16542		
22	33680	Jean-Pierre	Santa	1300	9987		
23	31509	Karpov	Linda	1000	9876		
24	83229	Kuang	Winnie	800	11356		
25	31825	Lee	Jun Yi	900	10325		
26	31988	Mang	Zhu Na	500	10789		
27	69978	Merzell	Fadhylla	1500	13654		
28	33680	Michaels	Ruzanna	600	14210		
29	31509	Narovlianski	Andy	700	10236		
30	83229	Ng	Gloria	900	13546		
31	35785	Phillips	Leanne	1000	16987		
32	32765	Saballos	Maria	1100	14569		
33	24401	St. Juste	Candace	1300	12547		
34	77984	Sultana	Zorina	700	11234		
35	10343	Wu	Sze Wai	2000	25369		
36	47957	Wu	Hao Ting	500	10459		
37	89334	Yassin	Sherin	900	11236		
38	15359	Yip	Miao Xian	1100	15645		
39	93280	Young	Tamara	1400	16875		
40	32585	Yuen	San San	1300	18987		
41							
42	TOTALS						
43	AVERAGE						
44	MAXIMUM						
45	MINIMUM						
46							

ACTIVITY 26: ACCOUNTS PAYABLE

New Skills Reinforced:

In this activity, you will practice how to:
1. format cells to percents.

Activity Overview:

Assume you work at your local mall at a fragrance boutique. Suppliers generally offer customers who buy on account a cash discount for early payment. For the buyer, the discount is called a purchase discount. For the seller, it is called a sales discount. The owner ordered many bottles of perfume for the Christmas season and will receive a discount if she pays her bills within 15 days. The owner asked you to help calculate what she owes to her vendors using a spreadsheet.

The following activity illustrates how spreadsheets can be used to calculate a small company's purchase discounts and sales tax.

Instructions:

1. Create a NEW spreadsheet.

   Note: Unless otherwise stated, the font should be set to Arial, the font size to 10 point.
2. Type the data as shown.
3. Format the width of column A to 24.0 and left align.
4. Format the width of column B to 11.0 and right align.
5. Format cells B10 – B40 as numbers displaying 2 decimal places.
6. Format the width of column C to 11.0 and center align.
7. **NEW SKILL** Format cells C10 – C35 as percentages displaying 0 decimal places.
8. Format the width of columns D – G to 11.0 and right align.
9. Format cells D10 – G40 as numbers displaying 2 decimal places.
10. Bold cell A2 and change the font size to 14 point.
11. Bold cell A3 and change the font size to 12 point.
12. Bold rows 7 and 8.
13. Compute the formulas for the first company, Baby Phat, as follows:
    a. PURCHASE DISCOUNT=AMOUNT OWED*% DISCOUNT -> In cell D10, type =B10*C10
    b. SUBTOTAL=AMOUNT OWED-PURCHASE DISCOUNT -> In cell E10, type =B10-D10
    c. SALES TAX=6%*SUBTOTAL -> In cell F10, type =6%*E10
    d. AMOUNT OWED=SUBTOTAL+SALES TAX -> In cell G10, type =E10+F10
14. Use the AutoFill feature to copy the formulas down for the remaining companies.
15. Enter formulas to calculate the Totals, Average, Maximum, and Minimum for column B and columns D – G.
16. Bold rows 37 – 40.
17. Display formulas in your spreadsheet by using <CTRL> + ` to check for accuracy.

18. Carefully proofread your work for accuracy.
19. Save the spreadsheet as ACCOUNTS PAYABLE.
20. Analyze the changes made to the data in the spreadsheet.
21. Set the Print Area to include all cells containing data in the spreadsheet.
22. Print Preview and adjust the Page Setup so that the spreadsheet fits on one page.
23. Print a copy of the spreadsheet if required by your instructor.

ACTIVITY 26: ACCOUNTS PAYABLE DATA SPREADSHEET

	A	B	C	D	E	F	G
1	Activity 26 Student Name						
2	CUSTOM FRAGRANCES						
3	Phipps Plaza Mall						
4	3500 Peachtree Rd NE # 11						
5	Atlanta, GA 30326						
6							
7		AMOUNT	%	PURCHASE			AMOUNT
8	COMPANY	OWED	DISCOUNT	DISCOUNT	SUBTOTAL	SALES TAX	OWED
9							
10	Baby Phat	658	0.03				
11	Boucheron	325	0.04				
12	Brittany Spears	1228	0.05				
13	Burberry of London	357	0.03				
14	Cacharel	421	0.02				
15	Calvin Klein	763	0.04				
16	Chanel	632	0.03				
17	Christian Dior	288	0.02				
18	Dolce & Gabanna	324	0.02				
19	Donald Trump	1056	0.05				
20	Donna Karan	1236	0.06				
21	Elizabeth Taylor	478	0.04				
22	Estee Lauder	631	0.07				
23	Georgio Armani	712	0.04				
24	Givenchy	284	0.02				
25	Gucci	394	0.03				
26	Guess?	578	0.04				
27	Hugo Boss	435	0.05				
28	Jennifer Lopez Fragrances	875	0.07				
29	Kenneth Cole	627	0.04				
30	Maria Sharapova	937	0.04				
31	Oscar de la Renta	765	0.04				
32	Paris Hilton	1181	0.02				
33	Ralph Lauren	654	0.03				
34	Sarah Jessica Parker	473	0.05				
35	Tommy Bahama	684	0.04				
36							
37	TOTALS						
38	AVERAGE						
39	MAXIMUM						
40	MINIMUM						

ACTIVITY 27: SAN ANTONIO SPURS® 2

New Skills Reinforced:

In this activity, you will practice how to:

1. cut, copy, and paste data.
2. use sets of parentheses in formulas.

Activity Overview:

This activity expands on the San Antonio Spurs® spreadsheet created in Activity 4.

This activity illustrates how spreadsheets can be used to record:

1. the players, their uniform numbers, their position, and games played.
2. field goals made, attempted, and percentage.
3. three-point shots made, attempted, and percentage.
4. free throws made, attempted, and percentage.
5. total points scored and scoring average.

Instructions:

1. Open the file SAN ANTONIO SPURS previously created in Activity 4.

   Note: Unless otherwise stated, the font should be set to Arial, the font size to 10 point.
2. Change the Activity # in row 1 to read Activity 27.
3. Type the additional data as shown in columns E – O.
4. NEW SKILL ▶ Copy cell A2 to cells E2 and K2.
5. NEW SKILL ▶ Cut cell A4 and paste it to cell E4.
6. Format the width of columns D – O to 7.0 and left align.
7. Format columns G, J, and M as percentages displaying 1 decimal place.
8. Compute the formulas for the first player as follows (*See Table 1-27 to interpret the abbreviations used in each column*):
   a. PCT (Percentage of field goals made)=FGM/FGA -> In cell G13, type =E13/F13
   b. PCT (Percentage of three-point shots made)=3PM/3PA -> In cell J13, type =H13/I13
   c. PCT (Percentage of free throws made)=FTM/FTA -> In cell M13, type =K13/L13
   d. NEW SKILL ▶ PTS (Total points scored)=(FGM*2)+(3PM*3)+FTM ->
      In cell N13, type =(E13*2)+(H13*3)+K13
   e. AVG (Average points per game)=PTS/GAMES PLAYED -> In cell O13, type =N13/D13
9. Use the AutoFill feature to copy the formulas down for the remaining players.
10. Display formulas in your spreadsheet by using <CTRL> + ` to check for accuracy.
11. Carefully proofread your work for accuracy.
12. Save the spreadsheet as SAN ANTONIO SPURS 2.
13. Analyze the changes made to the data in the spreadsheet.
14. Set the Print Area to include all cells containing data in the spreadsheet.
15. Print Preview and adjust the Page Setup so that the spreadsheet fits on one page. Set the page orientation to landscape.
16. Print a copy of the spreadsheet if required by your instructor.

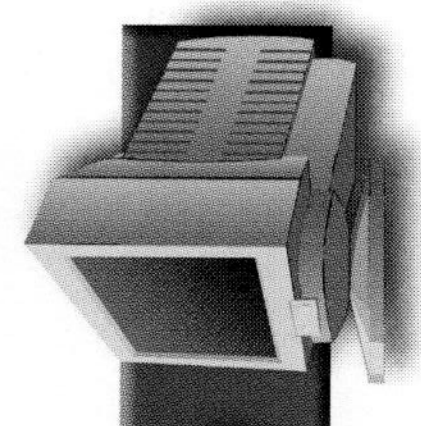

	A	B	C	D	E	F	G	H	I	J	K	L	M	N	O
1	Activity 27 Student Name														
2	**N.B.A. CHAMPIONS**														
3	**SAN ANTONIO SPURS**														
4	**2004-05 ROSTER**														
5															
6	Head Coach: Greg Popovich														
7															
8															
9															
10		**JERSEY**	**POSITION**	**GAMES**											
11	**PLAYER**	**NUMBER**	**PLAYED**	**PLAYED**	**FGM**	**FGA**	**PCT**	**3PM**	**3PA**	**PCT**	**FTM**	**FTA**	**PCT**	**PTS**	**AVG**
12															
13	Tim Duncan	21	F, C	66	517	1042		3	9		305	455			
14	Tony Parker	9	G	80	539	1118		43	156		210	323			
15	Manu Ginobili	20	G	74	367	780		97	258		355	442			
16	Glenn Robinson	3	F	9	34	77		2	6		20	23			
17	Bruce Bowen	12	F	82	251	498		102	253		71	112			
18	Brent Barry	17	G	81	194	459		100	280		113	135			
19	Devin Brown	23	G	67	173	409		45	121		103	130			
20	Nazr Mohammed	2	C	23	55	142		0	1		32	56			
21	Robert Horry	5	F, C	75	157	375		51	138		86	109			
22	Beno Udrih	14	G	80	173	390		58	142		67	89			
23	Rasho Nesterovic	8	C	70	198	430		0	1		14	30			
24	Dion Glover	9	G, F	7	8	22		1	8		8	10			
25	Sean Marks	40	F, C	23	27	80		0	3		22	28			
26	Tony Massenburg	34	F, C	61	74	182		0	1		48	63			
27	Mike Wilks	29	G	48	32	77		5	16		12	16			
28	Linton Johnson III	43	F	2	0	2		0	1		1	2			

Source: http://aol.nba.com/spurs/stats/2004/index.html

Table 1-27

Abbreviations interpreted:

FGM	Field Goals Made	FTM	Free Throws Made
FGA	Field Goals Attempted	FTA	Free Throws Attempted
3PM	Three-Point Shots Made	PTS	Total Points Scored
3PA	Three-Point Shots Attempted	AVG	Average Points Per Game

ACTIVITY 28: QUARTERBACK STATISTICS

New Skills Reinforced:

In this activity, you will practice how to:

1. change cell shading.

Activity Overview:

Statistics play an important role in any sport. They are used in evaluating team performance as well as the performance of individual players. Football statistics are very simple to understand and compute.

The following activity illustrates how spreadsheets can be used to compute the completion percentage of NFL® quarterbacks during the 2005 season. In this activity, you will be applying cell shading to enhance the appearance of a spreadsheet.

Instructions:

1. Create a NEW spreadsheet.

   Note: Unless otherwise stated, the font should be set to Arial, the font size to 10 point.
2. Type the data as shown.
3. Bold cell A2 and change the font size to 16 point.
4. Format the width of columns B and C to 20.0 and left align.
5. Center align cells A5 – A30 and cells D5 – G30.
6. Compute the formula for the first player's PCT (Completion Percentage) as follows:
   a. PCT(Completion Percentage)=Cmp(Completed Passes)/Att(Attempted Passes) ->

      In cell G7, type =F7/E7
7. Use the AutoFill feature to copy the formula down for PCT for the remaining players.
8. Format cells G7 – G30 as percentages displaying 1 decimal place.
9. **NEW SKILL** Change the shading for cells A5 – G5 to gray (25%).
10. Bold row 5.
11. Display formulas in your spreadsheet by using <CTRL> + ` to check for accuracy.
12. Carefully proofread your work for accuracy.
13. Save the spreadsheet as QUARTERBACK STATISTICS.
14. Analyze the changes made to the data in the spreadsheet.
15. Set the Print Area to include all cells containing data in the spreadsheet.
16. Print Preview and adjust the Page Setup so that the spreadsheet fits on one page.
17. Print a copy of the spreadsheet if required by your instructor.

ACTIVITY 28: QUARTERBACK STATISTICS DATA SPREADSHEET

	A	B	C	D	E	F	G
1	Activity 28 Student Name						
2	NFL 2005 QUARTERBACK STATISTICS						
3							
4							
5	RANK	PLAYER	TEAM	YDS	ATT	CMP	PCT
6							
7	1	Peyton Manning	Indianapolis Colts	3747	453	305	
8	2	Carson Palmer	Cincinnati Bengals	3836	509	345	
9	3	Ben Roethlisberger	Pittsburgh Steelers	2385	268	168	
10	4	Matt Hasselbeck	Seattle Seahawks	3459	449	294	
11	5	Marc Bulger	St. Louis Rams	2297	287	192	
12	6	Tom Brady	New England Patriots	4110	530	334	
13	7	Jake Plummer	Denver Broncos	3366	456	277	
14	8	Trent Green	Kansas City Chiefs	4014	507	317	
15	9	Byron Leftwich	Jacksonville Jaguars	2123	302	175	
16	10	Drew Brees	San Diego Chargers	3576	500	323	
17	11	Brad Johnson	Minnesota Vikings	1885	294	184	
18	12	Jake Delhomme	Carolina Panthers	3421	435	262	
19	13	Mark Brunell	Washington Redskins	3050	454	262	
20	14	Kurt Warner	Arizona Cardinals	2713	375	242	
21	15	Donovan McNabb	Philadelphia Eagles	2507	357	211	
22	16	Drew Bledsoe	Dallas Cowboys	3639	499	300	
23	17	Steve McNair	Tennessee Titans	3161	476	292	
24	18	Chris Simms	Tampa Bay Buccaneers	2035	313	191	
25	19	Kerry Collins	Oakland Raiders	3759	565	302	
26	20	David Carr	Houston Texans	2488	423	256	
27	21	Trent Dilfer	Cleveland Browns	2321	333	199	
28	22	Eli Manning	New York Giants	3762	557	294	
29	23	Michael Vick	Atlanta Falcons	2412	387	214	
30	24	Brett Favre	Green Bay Packers	3881	607	372	

Source: www.NFL.com

ACTIVITY 29: RECIPES

New Skills Reinforced:

In this activity, you will practice how to:
1. format cells as fractions.

Activity Overview:

Assume that you are a culinary arts student. Your teacher has asked you to search the Internet for cookie and brownie recipes. She then asks you to type them up so you can distribute them to your classmates. You decide to type them using Microsoft Excel®. You notice that every time you type "½," Microsoft Excel® changes it to "2-Jan."

The following activity illustrates how spreadsheets can be used to format cells as fractions.

Instructions:

1. Create a NEW spreadsheet.

   Note: Unless otherwise stated, the font should be set to Arial, the font size to 10 point.

2. Type the data as shown.
3. Bold cells A2, A6, and A20 and change the font size to 16 point.
4. Bold and underline rows 8 and 22.
5. Format the width of column A to 36.0.
6. Format the width of columns B and C to 16.0 and center align.
7. **NEW SKILL** Format column B as fractions, up to one digit.
8. Carefully proofread your work for accuracy.
9. Save the spreadsheet as RECIPES.
10. Analyze the changes made to the data in the spreadsheet.
11. Set the Print Area to include all cells containing data in the spreadsheet.
12. Print Preview and adjust the Page Setup so that the spreadsheet fits on one page.
13. Print a copy of the spreadsheet if required by your instructor.

ACTIVITY 29: RECIPES DATA SPREADSHEET

	A	B	C
1	Activity 29 Student Name		
2	RECIPES		
3			
4			
5			
6	Chocolate Chip Cookies		
7			
8	INGREDIENTS	AMOUNT	MEASUREMENT
9	flour	2.25	cup
10	baking soda	1	teaspoon
11	margarine	0.5	cup
12	white sugar	0.25	cup
13	light brown sugar	0.75	cup
14	vanilla extract	1	teaspoon
15	package instant vanilla pudding mix	3.5	ounce
16	eggs	2	large
17	chocolate chips	1.5	cup
18			
19			
20	Blondie Brownies		
21			
22	INGREDIENTS	AMOUNT	MEASUREMENT
23	shortening	0.5	cup
24	milk	1.5	tablespoon
25	brown sugar	0.5	cup
26	egg	1	large
27	flour	1.5	cup
28	baking powder	0.5	teaspoon
29	salt	0.125	teaspoon
30	vanilla extract	1	teaspoon
31	chopped walnuts	0.5	cup

ACTIVITY 30: NBA® STANDINGS

New Skills Reinforced:

In this activity, you will practice how to:
1. insert and delete rows.

Activity Overview:

The National Basketball Association® (NBA®) is one of the most popular professional sports leagues in the world! It is estimated that the American game is now played by more than 250 million people worldwide in an organized fashion, as well as by countless others in "pick-up" games.

In the regular season, each NBA® team plays 82 games, which are divided evenly between home and away games. Schedules are not identical for all teams. A team faces opponents in its own division four times a year, teams from the other two divisions in its conference either three or four times a year, and teams in the other conference two times each.

The following activity illustrates how newspapers use spreadsheets to list the NBA® Standings so sports enthusiasts can see how their favorite teams are doing as compared to other teams in the NBA®.

Instructions:

1. Create a NEW spreadsheet.
   Note: Unless otherwise stated, the font should be set to Arial, the font size to 10 point.
2. Type the data as shown.
3. **NEW SKILL** Delete rows 5 and 28 simultaneously (**Hint:** Click and hold <CTRL> to select both rows).
4. **NEW SKILL** Insert a row above EASTERN CONFERENCE.
5. Format the width of column A to 26.0 and columns B – E to 8.0.
6. Bold row 2 and change the font size to 16 point.
7. Bold rows 5 and 27 and change the font size to 14 point.
8. Bold rows 6, 13, 20, 28, 35, and 42 and change the font size to 12 point.
9. Compute the formula for PCT (Percentage Won) for the first game as follows:
   a. PCT(Percentage Won)=W/(W+L) -> (**Note:** *W(Wins), L(Losses)*)
      In cell D7, type =B7/(B7+C7)

   Note: You will compute the GB (Games Back) column in Activity 51.
10. Copy and paste the PCT formula in cell D7 for the remaining teams in each division in column D.
11. Format column D as numbers displaying 3 decimal places.
12. Center align columns B – E.
13. Display formulas in your spreadsheet by using <CTRL> + ` to check for accuracy.
14. Carefully proofread your work for accuracy.
15. Save the spreadsheet as NBA STANDINGS.
16. Analyze the changes made to the data in the spreadsheet.
17. Set the Print Area to include all cells containing data in the spreadsheet.
18. Print Preview and adjust the Page Setup so that the spreadsheet fits on one page.
19. Print a copy of the spreadsheet if required by your instructor.

ACTIVITY 30: NBA® STANDINGS DATA SPREADSHEET

	A	B	C	D	E
1	Activity 30 Student Name				
2	N.B.A. STANDINGS		2005-2006 Division Standings		
3					
4	EASTERN CONFERENCE				
5					
6	ATLANTIC DIVISION	W	L	PCT	GB
7	New Jersey Nets	49	33		
8	Philadelphia 76ers	38	44		
9	Boston Celtics	33	49		
10	Toronto Raptors	27	55		
11	New York Knicks	23	59		
12					
13	CENTRAL DIVISION	W	L	PCT	GB
14	Detroit Pistons	64	18		
15	Cleveland Cavaliers	50	32		
16	Indiana Pacers	41	41		
17	Chicago Bulls	41	41		
18	Milwaukee Bucks	40	42		
19					
20	SOUTHEAST DIVISION	W	L	PCT	GB
21	Miami Heat	52	30		
22	Washington Wizards	42	40		
23	Orlando Magic	36	46		
24	Charlotte Bobcats	26	56		
25	Atlanta Hawks	26	56		
26					
27	WESTERN CONFERENCE				
28					
29	NORTHWEST DIVISION	W	L	PCT	GB
30	Denver Nuggets	44	38		
31	Utah Jazz	41	41		
32	Seattle SuperSonics	35	47		
33	Minnesota Timberwolves	33	49		
34	Portland Trail Blazers	21	61		
35					
36	PACIFIC DIVISION	W	L	PCT	GB
37	Phoenix Suns	54	28		
38	L.A. Clippers	47	35		
39	L.A. Lakers	45	37		
40	Sacramento Kings	44	38		
41	Golden State Warriors	34	48		
42					
43	SOUTHWEST DIVISION	W	L	PCT	GB
44	San Antonio Spurs	63	19		
45	Dallas Mavericks	60	22		
46	Memphis Grizzlies	49	33		
47	New Orleans Hornets	38	44		
48	Houston Rockets	34	48		

Source: www.NBA.com

ACTIVITY 31: OLD NAVY® SALES

New Skills Reinforced:

In this activity, you will practice how to:

1. use the absolute cell reference in a formula.

Activity Overview:

Gap® Inc. opened the first three Old Navy® stores in 1994, in the Northern California cities of Colma, San Leandro, and Pittsburg. Old Navy's® mission is to offer affordable, fashionable clothing and accessories for the whole family. Their merchandise is sold under the Old Navy® name in their stores and on their Web site.

The following activity illustrates how spreadsheets can be used to calculate percent of sales for each department as it relates to the total sales for the week.

Instructions:

1. Create a NEW spreadsheet.
   Note: Unless otherwise stated, the font should be set to Arial, the font size to 10 point.
2. Type the data as shown.
3. Bold cell A2 and change the font size to 16 point.
4. Bold and underline rows 12 and 35.
5. Bold cell E11.
6. Format the width of column A to 20.0 and left align.
7. Format the width of columns B – D to 15.0 and right align.
8. Format cells B14 – D35 as numbers displaying 2 decimal places.
9. Format the width of column E to 15.0 and right align.
10. Format cells E14 – E35 as percentages displaying 2 decimal places.
11. Compute the total for column B, SALES -> In cell B35, type =SUM(B14:B33)
12. Compute the formulas for the first department as follows:
    a. TAX=8.625%*SALES -> In cell C14, type =8.625%*B14
    b. TOTAL=SALES+TAX -> In cell D14, type =B14+C14
    c. % OF SALES=SALES/TOTAL SALES -> In cell E14, type =B14/$B$35 (NEW SKILL)
    Note: The dollar signs in the % OF SALES formula generates the absolute cell reference.
13. Use the AutoFill feature to copy the formulas down for the remaining departments.
14. Enter formulas to total columns C – E.
15. Display formulas in your spreadsheet by using <CTRL> + ` to check for accuracy.
16. Carefully proofread your work for accuracy.
17. Save the spreadsheet as OLD NAVY SALES.
18. Analyze the changes made to the data in the spreadsheet.
19. Set the Print Area to include all cells containing data in the spreadsheet.
20. Print Preview and adjust the Page Setup so that the spreadsheet fits on one page.
21. Print a copy of the spreadsheet if required by your instructor.

ACTIVITY 31: OLD NAVY® SALES DATA SPREADSHEET

	A	B	C	D	E
1	Activity 31 Student Name				
2	OLD NAVY				
3	FLATBUSH CENTER				
4	1009 Flatbush Avenue				
5	Brooklyn, NY 11226				
6					
7					
8	Girl's Department Sales Breakdown				
9	December 18 - 24, 2005				
10					
11					% OF
12	DEPARTMENT	SALES	TAX	TOTAL	SALES
13					
14	New Arrivals	2123.54			
15	Glam Central	1287.63			
16	Shop By Outfit	1689.36			
17	Wear to Work	1065.21			
18	Tees & Camis	1547.36			
19	Pants	1637.36			
20	Top Trends	1345.32			
21	Graphic Tees	1547.43			
22	Skirts & Dresses	1897.12			
23	Shirts	1776.04			
24	Outerwear	1893.78			
25	Activewear	1987.85			
26	Sweaters	1569.45			
27	Jeans & Cords	1383.12			
28	Sleepwear & Intimates	1024.98			
29	Shoes	2436.78			
30	Tanks & Polos	1532.25			
31	Outfits	1931.45			
32	Shorts & Capris	1828.91			
33	Accessories	1732.28			
34					
35	TOTALS				

Source: www.OldNavy.com

ACTIVITY 32: AMAZON.COM® MUSIC

New Skills Reinforced:

In this activity, you will practice how to:
1. format font colors.

Activity Overview:

Amazon.com® was founded by Jeff Bezos in 1994 and was first launched in 1995. The company today serves more than 30 million customers and employs more than 7,000 people in many countries. Not only has Amazon.com® managed to become a profitable e-commerce business, but it has also pioneered the online shopping technology most e-commerce stores utilize today.

Amazon.com® offers a wide range of goods for sale to any consumer who has access to a computer and the Internet. Amazon.com® offers products from a range of manufacturers in one convenient location. It serves its suppliers by purchasing products to sell on its Web site to Amazon customers. Manufacturers and suppliers now have a new outlet to sell their goods, which increases their revenue stream.

The following activity illustrates how spreadsheets can be used to list customer discounts. In this example, the product category used is music.

Instructions:

1. Create a NEW spreadsheet.
   Note: Unless otherwise stated, the font should be set to Arial, the font size to 10 point.
2. Type the data as shown.
3. Bold cell A2 and change the font size to 14 point.
4. Bold rows 5 and 6.
5. Format the width of columns A and B to 30.0 and left align.
6. Format the width of columns C – E to 12.0 and right align.
7. Format cells C8 – C27 as currency displaying 2 decimal places and the $ symbol.
8. Format the width of column F to 12.0 and right align.
9. Format cells F8 – F27 as percentages displaying 0 decimals.
10. Compute the formulas for the first album as follows:
    a. YOU SAVE=LIST PRICE-OUR PRICE -> In cell E8, type =C8-D8
    b. % OF SAVINGS=YOU SAVE/LIST PRICE -> In cell F8, type =E8/C8
11. Use the AutoFill feature to copy the formulas down for the remaining albums.
12. NEW SKILL For column F, % OF SAVINGS, change the font color to red for all cells whose percentage values are greater than or equal to 25%.
13. Display formulas in your spreadsheet by using <CTRL> + ` to check for accuracy.
14. Carefully proofread your work for accuracy.
15. Save the spreadsheet as AMAZON MUSIC.
16. Analyze the changes made to the data in the spreadsheet.
17. Set the Print Area to include all cells containing data in the spreadsheet.
18. Print Preview and adjust the Page Setup so that the spreadsheet fits on one page.
19. Print a copy of the spreadsheet if required by your instructor.

ACTIVITY 32: AMAZON.COM® MUSIC DATA SPREADSHEET

	A	B	C	D	E	F
1	Activity 32 Student Name					
2	AMAZON MUSIC					
3	Top Sellers November 2005					
4						
5			LIST	OUR	YOU	% OF
6	ARTIST	ALBUM	PRICE	PRICE	SAVE	SAVINGS
7						
8	Madonna	Confessions on a Dance Floor	18.98	10.99		
9	Carrie Underwood	Some Hearts	17.98	10.49		
10	Kelly Clarkson	Breakaway	18.98	13.29		
11	Green Day	American Idiot	18.98	13.49		
12	Black Eyed Peas	Monkey Business	13.98	10.99		
13	Sheryl Crow	Wildflower	13.98	11.99		
14	Alicia Keys	Unplugged	18.98	13.99		
15	Eminem	Curtain Call	13.98	10.98		
16	Alanis Morissette	The Collection	18.98	13.99		
17	Stevie Wonder	A Time to Love	13.98	11.99		
18	Notorious B.I.G.	Duets	18.98	14.99		
19	Mary J. Blige	The Breakthrough	13.98	12.99		
20	Jamie Foxx	Unpredictable	18.98	10.99		
21	Kanye West	Late Registration	13.98	12.99		
22	Lindsay Lohan	A Little More Personal	13.98	12.49		
23	Destiny's Child	#1's Dual Disc	18.99	13.29		
24	Tony Braxton	Libra	13.98	12.99		
25	Chris Brown	Chris Brown	18.98	10.98		
26	Ginuwine	Back 2 Basics	18.98	14.99		
27	Ray J	Raydiation	18.98	14.99		

Source: www.amazon.com

ACTIVITY 33: TOP 10 DVDS

New Skills Reinforced:

In this activity, you will practice how to:
1. insert columns.
2. move columns.

Activity Overview:

The retail market for DVDs has skyrocketed in the last few years. One of the country's premier booksellers, Barnes & Noble®, has joined the DVD business. Barnes & Noble® (www.bn.com), the Internet's largest bookseller, now offers over 40,000 DVD titles. The customer-friendly Web site has become a favorite among movie lovers and offers discounts on many titles. They offer affordable shipping charges and even provide same day shipping to many cities within the U.S.

The following activity illustrates how spreadsheets can be used to list the top 10 bestselling DVDs for a major retailer.

Instructions:

1. Create a NEW spreadsheet.
   Note: Unless otherwise stated, the font should be set to Arial, the font size to 10 point.
2. Type the data as shown.
3. Bold cell A1 and change the font size to 18 point.
4. Bold cell A2 and change the font size to 14 point.
5. Format the width of column A to 10.0 and left align.
6. Format the width of column B to 25.0 and left align.
7. Center align, bold, and underline row 4.
8. Format the width of columns C – G to 15.0.
9. Format cells C5 – C14 as dates showing mm/dd/yyyy.
10. Use the AutoFill feature to complete the numbering sequence in column A to RANK the movies.
11. Compute the formulas for the first movie as follows:
    a. B&N DISCOUNT=LIST PRICE*30% -> In cell E5, type =D5*30%
    b. B&N PRICE=LIST PRICE-B&N DISCOUNT -> In cell F5, type =D5-E5
12. Use the AutoFill feature to copy the formulas down for the remaining movies.

NEW SKILL

13. Insert a column between column B, TITLE, and column C, RELEASE DATE. Then, move the RATING column to the newly created column. The RATING data should now be in column C.
14. Format columns E – G as currency displaying 2 decimal places and the $ symbol.
15. Insert a header that shows:
    a. Left Section Activity 33-Student Name
    b. Center Section TOP 10 DVDS
    c. Right Section Current Date

16. Insert a footer that shows:
    a. Center Section PAGE number
17. Display formulas in your spreadsheet by using <CTRL> + ` to check for accuracy.
18. Carefully proofread your work for accuracy.
19. Save the spreadsheet as TOP 10 DVDS.
20. Analyze the changes made to the data in the spreadsheet.
21. Set the Print Area to include all cells containing data in the spreadsheet.
22. Print Preview and adjust the Page Setup so that the spreadsheet fits on one page. Set the page orientation to landscape.
23. Print a copy of the spreadsheet if required by your instructor.

ACTIVITY 33: TOP 10 DVDS DATA SPREADSHEET

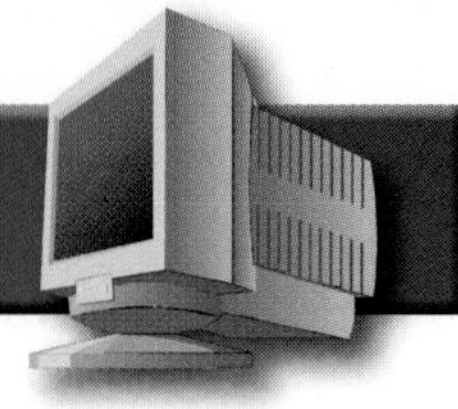

	A	B	C	D	E	F	G
1	Top 10 DVD Bestsellers						
2	Barnes & Noble						
3							
4	RANK	TITLE	RELEASE DATE	LIST PRICE	B&N DISCOUNT	B&N PRICE	RATING
5	1	The Princess Bride	9/4/01	14.98			G
6	2	Must Love Dogs	12/20/05	14.98			PG-13
7		My Big Fat Greek Wedding	2/11/03	14.98			PG
8		Shakespeare in Love	12/7/99	14.98			R
9		Love Actually	4/27/04	14.98			R
10		The Chronicles of Narnia	4/4/06	27.98			PG
11		Strictly Ballroom	3/19/02	14.98			PG
12		The Very Hungry Caterpillar	1/3/06	14.98			NR
13		The Matrix	9/21/99	14.98			R
14		Emma	1/5/99	14.98			PG

Source: www.bn.com

ACTIVITY 34: EXPENSE REPORT

New Skills Reinforced:

In this activity, you will practice how to:
1. insert a page break in a spreadsheet.

Activity Overview:

Many companies send their employees on business trips. Companies will reimburse their staff for expenses incurred in the performance of their job. Travel and other personal expenses can be reimbursed only by submitting a properly completed and approved expense report. This report must be accompanied by original receipts and paid invoices. Travel claims usually are submitted within 30 working days following the completion of each trip. Reports that are not properly completed will be returned to the claimant or the supervisor for clarification.

The following activity illustrates how spreadsheets can be used to create employee expense reports. Please note that when employees use their own cars to conduct on-the-job duties, they are usually reimbursed a certain amount per each mile driven. In this example, the employee is reimbured 40.5 cents per mile.

Instructions:

1. Create a NEW spreadsheet.
   Note: Unless otherwise stated, the font should be set to Arial, the font size to 10 point.
2. Type the data as shown. To save time, copy and paste the data in cells A1 – A23 to cells A28 – A50.
3. Enter your name as the employee in cells B7 and B34.
4. Format the width of column A to 22.0 and left align.
5. Format the width of columns B – G to 10.0 and right align.
6. Bold rows 1, 5, 7, 23, 28, 32, 34, and 50.
7. Bold and underline rows 11 and 38.
8. Compute the TOTAL for Car Miles in the first expense report as follows:
   In cell G13, type =SUM(B13:F13)*0.405
9. In cells G14 – G21, enter SUM formulas to compute the totals for the remaining expenses.
10. Compute the TOTAL for Car Miles in the second expense report as follows:
    In cell G40, type =SUM(B40:F40)*0.405
11. In cells G41 - G48, enter SUM formulas to compute the totals for the remaining expenses.
12. In cells G23 and G50, use the AutoSum feature to compute the total expense for each expense report.
13. Bold column G.
14. **NEW SKILL** At cell A28, insert a Page Break. This will force the two expense reports to print on separate pages.
15. Display formulas in your spreadsheet by using <CTRL> + ` to check for accuracy.
16. Carefully proofread your work for accuracy.
17. Save the spreadsheet as EXPENSE REPORT.

Activity 34: Expense Report Instructions Continued

18. Analyze the changes made to the data in the spreadsheet.
19. Set the Print Area to include all cells containing data in the spreadsheet.
20. Print Preview and adjust the Page Setup so that each expense report fits on its own page.
21. Print a copy of each expense report if required by your instructor.

ACTIVITY 34: EXPENSE REPORT DATA SPREADSHEET

	A	B	C	D	E	F	G
1	CASTLETON AGENCY		Activity 34 Student Name				
2	1910 S Jamestown Avenue						
3	Tulsa, OK 74112						
4							
5	EXPENSE REPORT						
6							
7	EMPLOYEE NAME:	Student Name					
8							
9							
10							
11	EXPENSES	11/6/2006	11/7/2006	11/8/2006	11/9/2006	11/10/2006	TOTALS
12							
13	Car Miles @ $0.405	212	54	48	46	230	
14	Hotel	123.28	123.28	123.28	123.28	0.00	
15	Breakfast	0.00	11.86	13.82	11.28	17.36	
16	Lunch	22.32	18.96	65.21	75.32	26.11	
17	Dinner	36.54	128.32	245.88	45.36	0.00	
18	Entertainment	69.36	123.25	48.35	156.78	0.00	
19	Dry Cleaning	0.00	24.00	0.00	18.00	0.00	
20	Printing	86.32	0.00	0.00	48.25	0.00	
21	Misc.	0.00	11.36	14.30	0.00	12.36	
22							
23	TOTAL						
24							
25							
26							
27							
28	CASTLETON AGENCY		Activity 34 Student Name				
29	1910 S Jamestown Avenue						
30	Tulsa, OK 74112						
31							
32	EXPENSE REPORT						
33							
34	EMPLOYEE NAME:	Student Name					
35							
36							
37							
38	EXPENSES	12/4/2006	12/5/2006	12/6/2006	12/7/2006	12/8/2006	TOTALS
39							
40	Car Miles @ $0.405	321	89	78	106	412	
41	Hotel	146.37	146.37	146.37	146.37	0.00	
42	Breakfast	0.00	15.36	18.54	12.36	65.35	
43	Lunch	42.36	28.36	125.32	28.26	15.23	
44	Dinner	65.32	254.36	22.36	225.36	0.00	
45	Entertainment	25.36	0.00	0.00	45.36	0.00	
46	Dry Cleaning	45.00	0.00	0.00	15.00	0.00	
47	Printing	0.00	0.00	0.00	128.04	0.00	
48	Misc.	10.00	0.00	12.89	0.00	6.36	
49							
50	TOTAL						

ACTIVITY 35: PERSONAL CD COLLECTION

New Skills Reinforced:

In this activity, you will practice how to:
1. delete columns.
2. use <CTRL>+D to duplicate data in cells.

Activity Overview:

For many people, collecting albums and CDs becomes more than a hobby. When someone's collection begins to grow, it becomes obvious that there needs to be a way to properly catalog what they own. Creating a personal CD collection list can be quite helpful. Gathering information such as artist, album, genre, and a list of tracks makes it easy to find the song or CD you are looking for. Using a program like Microsoft Excel® allows a music lover to organize, sort, and search their compilation with just the click of the mouse.

The following activity illustrates how spreadsheets can be used to maintain a personal CD collection.

Instructions:

1. Create a NEW spreadsheet.

   Note: Unless otherwise stated, the font should be set to Arial, the font size to 10 point.
2. Type the data as shown.
3. NEW SKILL ▶ Delete the empty column D.
4. Format the width of columns A and C to 17.0.
5. Format the width of column B to 20.0 and column D to 30.0.
6. NEW SKILL ▶ Select cells A5 – C13 and duplicate the data by pressing <CTRL>+D. Repeat the same procedure for cells A16 – C27, A30 – C42, and A45 – C56.
7. Bold cell A1 and change the font size to 20 point.
8. Bold rows 4, 15, 29, and 44.
9. Insert a header that shows:
   a. Left Section — Activity 35-Student Name
   b. Center Section — PERSONAL CD COLLECTION
   c. Right Section — Current Date
10. Insert a footer that shows:
    a. Center Section — PAGE number
11. Carefully proofread your work for accuracy.
12. Save the spreadsheet as PERSONAL CD COLLECTION.
13. Analyze the changes made to the data in the spreadsheet.
14. Set the Print Area to include all cells containing data in the spreadsheet.
15. Print Preview and adjust the Page Setup so that the spreadsheet fits on one page.
16. Print a copy of the spreadsheet if required by your instructor.

ACTIVITY 35: PERSONAL CD COLLECTION DATA SPREADSHEET

	A	B	C	D	E	F	G
1		Personal CD Collection					
2							
3							
4	Genre	Artist	Album		Tracks		
5	Classic Rock	Dire Straits	Brothers in Arms		So Far Away		
6					Money for Nothing		
7					Walk of Life		
8					Your Latest Trick		
9					Why Worry		
10					Ride Across the River		
11					The Man's Too Strong		
12					One World		
13					Brother in Arms		
14							
15	Genre	Artist	Album		Tracks		
16	Alternative	Blink 182	Enema of the State		Dumpweed		
17					Don't Leave Me		
18					Aliens Exist		
19					Going Away To College		
20					What's My Age Again		
21					Dysentery Gary		
22					Adam's Song		
23					All The Small Things		
24					The Party Song		
25					Mutt		
26					Wendy Clear		
27					Anthem		
28							
29	Genre	Artist	Album		Tracks		
30	Alternative	Linkin Park	Meteora		Foreword		
31					Don't Stay		
32					Somewhere I Belong		
33					Lying From You		
34					Hit the Floor		
35					Easier to Run		
36					Faint		
37					Figure		
38					Breaking the Habit		
39					From the Inside		
40					Nobody's Listening		
41					Session		
42					Numb		
43							
44	Genre	Artist	Album		Tracks		
45	Alternative	Blues Traveler	Four		Run-Around		
46					Stand		
47					Look Around		
48					Fallible		
49					The Mountains Win Again		
50					Freedom		
51					Crash Burn		
52					Price To Pay		
53					Hook		
54					The Good, The Bad, And The Ugly		
55					Just Wait		
56					Brother John		

ACTIVITY 36: CAREERS

New Skills Reinforced:

In this activity, you will practice how to:

1. adjust page scaling so that multiple page data can print on one page.

Activity Overview:

Choosing a career is one of life's biggest decisions. With so many career choices to pick from, most students find it difficult to decide what they want to be when they grow up. Many students start their search with an interest inventory. An interest inventory asks questions that help organize a person's likes and dislikes regarding work and tasks. It also helps match a person's personality to different types of professions. Once a student narrows down the careers that seem to fit their characteristics, they can then begin researching those careers further and decide what might interest them. A Web site like skillchart.com is a great place to find out what skills a career requires.

The following activity illustrates how spreadsheets can be used to list the top 10 careers by personality traits.

Instructions:

1. Create a NEW spreadsheet.
   Note: Unless otherwise stated, the font should be set to Arial, the font size to 10 point.
2. Type the data as shown.
3. Bold cell A1 and change the font size to 16 point.
4. Bold row 3.
5. Use AutoFill to complete the sequence of numbered items in column A.
6. Change the column widths as follows:
   a. Column A to 8.0
   b. Column B to 22.0
   c. Column C to 38.0
   d. Column D to 30.0
   e. Column E to 26.0
   f. Column F to 28.0
   g. Column G to 26.0
7. Change the shading to 25% gray for cells A3 – A13, C3 – C13, E3 – E13, and G3 – G13.
8. Insert a header that shows:
   a. Left Section Activity 36-Student Name
   b. Center Section CAREERS
   c. Right Section Current Date
9. Insert a footer that shows:
   a. Center Section PAGE number
10. Carefully proofread your work for accuracy.
11. Save the spreadsheet as CAREERS.
12. Analyze the changes made to the data in the spreadsheet.
13. Set the Print Area to include all cells containing data in the spreadsheet.
14. NEW SKILL ▶ Print Preview and adjust the Page Setup so that the spreadsheet fits on one page. Adjust the scaling to 65% of normal size. Set the page orientation to landscape.
15. Print a copy of the spreadsheet if required by your instructor.

ACTIVITY 36: CAREERS DATA SPREADSHEET

	A	B	C	D
1	Top 10 Careers by Personality			
2				
3	Trait>	Like to Keep Learning	Want to make a lot of money	Dislike work place restrictions
4	1	Software Developer	Investment Banker	Computer Programmer
5	2	Physicist	Financial Analyst	Artist
6		Diplomat	Management Consultant	Writer
7		Journalist	Construction Manager	Actor
8		Architect	Banker	Petroleum Engineer
9		Benefits Administrator	Service Sales Representative (potentially)	Coach
10		Physician	Stockbroker	Philosopher
11		Computer Programmer	Court Reporter	Zoologist
12		Teacher	Carpenter	Anthropologist
13		Writer	Marketing Executive	Child Care Worker

	E	F	G
1			
2			
3	Have Type-A Personalities	Prefer Unpredictable Days	Love Working with People
4	Attorney	Detective/Private Investigator	Teacher
5	Investment Banker	FBI Agent	Human Resources Manager
6	Management Consultant	Police Officer	Guidance Counselor
7	Pilot	Restauranteur	Career Counselor
8	Military Officer	Firefighter	Psychologist
9	Architect	Musician	Social Worker
10	Baseball Player	Advertising Executive	Child Care Worker
11	Coach	Petroleum Engineer	Physical Therapist
12	Astronaut	Promoter	Fundraiser
13	Stockbroker	Agent	Hotel Manager

Source: http://www.skillchart.com/careers/top.htm

ACTIVITY 37: FIDELITY INVESTMENTS®

New Skills Reinforced:

In this activity, you will practice how to:
1. format cells to negative numbers.
2. change a cell's fill color.

Activity Overview:

A mutual fund is an open-ended fund operated by an investment company, such as Fidelity®, which raises money from shareholders and invests in a group of assets in accordance with a stated set of objectives. Mutual funds raise money by selling shares of the fund to the public, much like how other companies sell stock themselves to the public. Mutual funds then take the money they receive from the sale of their shares (along with any money made from previous investments) and use it to purchase various investment vehicles, such as stocks, bonds, and money market instruments.

Fidelity® is the world's largest mutual fund broker and offers a variety of mutual funds to the public. The following activity illustrates how spreadsheets can be used to determine gains or losses in mutual fund investments.

Instructions:

1. Create a NEW spreadsheet.

   Note: Unless otherwise stated, the font should be set to Arial, the font size to 10 point.
2. Type the data as shown.
3. Format the width of column A to 24.0 and left align.
4. Format the width of column B to 8.0 and left align.
5. Format the width of columns C – J to 11.0 and right align.
6. Format cells C1 – H1 as dates as showing mm/dd/yy.
7. NEW SKILL ▸ Format cells C4 – I20 as numbers displaying 2 decimal places. Set the negative numbers to red and to display parentheses.
8. Format cells J4 – J20 as percentages displaying 2 decimal places.
9. Bold rows 1 and 2.
10. Underline row 2.
11. Compute the formulas for the first fund as follows:
    a. 01/01/05 VALUE=01/01/05 PRICE*01/01/05 SHARES -> In cell E4, type =C4*D4
    b. 12/31/05 VALUE=12/31/05 PRICE*12/31/05 SHARES -> In cell H4, type =F4*G4
    c. $ GAIN/LOSS=12/31/05 VALUE-01/01/05 VALUE -> In cell I4, type =H4-E4
    d. % GAIN/LOSS=$ GAIN/LOSS / 01/01/05 VALUE -> In cell J4, type =I4/E4
12. Use the AutoFill feature to copy the formulas down for the remaining funds.
13. NEW SKILL ▸ Change the fill color for cells E1 – E20 and H1 – H20 to yellow.
14. NEW SKILL ▸ Change the fill color for cells I1 – I20 and J1 – J20 to light green.

15. Insert a header that shows:
    a. Left Section — Activity 37-Student Name
    b. Center Section — FIDELITY INVESTMENTS
    c. Right Section — Current Date
16. Insert a footer that shows:
    a. Center Section — PAGE number
17. Display formulas in your spreadsheet by using <CTRL> + ` to check for accuracy.
18. Carefully proofread your work for accuracy.
19. Save the spreadsheet as FIDELITY INVESTMENTS.
20. Analyze the changes made to the data in the spreadsheet.
21. Set the Print Area to include all cells containing data in the spreadsheet.
22. Print Preview and adjust the Page Setup so that the spreadsheet fits on one page. Set the page orientation to landscape.
23. Print a copy of the spreadsheet if required by your instructor.

ACTIVITY 37: FIDELITY INVESTMENTS® DATA SPREADSHEET

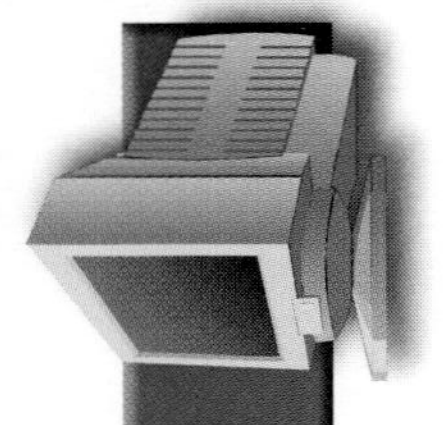

	A	B	C	D	E	F	G	H	I	J
1	FIDELITY	TICKER	01/01/05	01/01/05	01/01/05	12/31/05	12/31/05	12/31/05	$	%
2	FUND NAME	SYMBOL	PRICE	SHARES	VALUE	PRICE	SHARES	VALUE	GAIN/LOSS	GAIN/LOSS
3										
4	ASSET MANAGER	FASMX	16.20	165.32		16.05	166.97			
5	BALANCED	FBALX	17.82	156.58		18.76	159.71			
6	BLUE CHIP	FBCVX	12.55	154.32		13.50	157.41			
7	DESTINY I	FDESX	12.83	157.32		14.26	160.47			
8	DESTINY II	FDETX	11.92	147.35		11.89	147.35			
9	CAPITAL APPRECIATION	FDCAX	26.03	197.32		25.10	199.29			
10	DIVERSIFIED INTL.	FDIVX	28.64	132.45		32.54	132.45			
11	EQUITY INCOME	FEQIX	51.60	78.26		52.78	79.04			
12	EQUITY INCOME II	FEQTX	23.56	126.12		22.86	128.64			
13	EUROPE	FIEUX	34.11	123.45		35.97	124.68			
14	EXPORT	FEXPX	19.06	98.23		21.24	101.18			
15	FIDELITY	FFIDX	29.66	154.23		31.82	157.31			
16	GOVT BALANCED	FGBLX	20.99	123.26		21.06	123.26			
17	GROWTH COMPANY	FDGRX	56.06	83.21		63.63	83.21			
18	GROWTH AND INCOME	FGRIX	36.71	121.32		123.75	38.00			
19	HIGH INCOME	SPHIX	8.61	289.34		8.78	295.13			
20	INDEPENDENCE	FDFFX	17.82	128.32		19.65	132.17			

Source: www.fidelity.com

ACTIVITY 38: ABERCROMBIE & FITCH® 2

New Skills Reinforced:

In this activity, you will practice how to:

1. use the Count function.
2. use the AutoFormat feature.

Activity Overview:

The following activity illustrates how spreadsheets can be used by a retail clothing store that sells merchandise to the general public. Businesses must determine how inventory should be marked up by dollars and percents.

This activity expands on the Abercrombie & Fitch® spreadsheet created in Activity 7.

Instructions:

1. Open the file ABERCROMBIE & FITCH previously created in Activity 7.
   Note: Unless otherwise stated, the font should be set to Arial, the font size to 10 point.
2. Delete row 1 containing the Activity # and Student Name.
3. Type the additional column headings as shown for columns G and H. Bold these headings.
4. Center align columns G and H.
5. Type the additional data shown in cells A17 and A30.
6. Compute the formulas for the first item as follows:
   a. $ MARKUP=SELLING PRICE-UNIT COST -> In cell G8, type =F8-E8
   b. % MARKUP=$ MARKUP/UNIT COST -> In cell H8, type =G8/E8
7. Copy and paste these formulas for the remaining men's and women's wear items.
8. Format cells E8 – G29 as currency displaying 2 decimal places and the $ symbol.
9. Format cells H8 – H29 as percentages displaying 2 decimal places.

NEW SKILL ▶ 10. In cells B17 and B30, use the COUNT function to determine the number of items for men's wear and for women's wear. Enter the following formulas:
   a. In cell B17, type =COUNT(B8:B16)
   b. In cell B30, type =COUNT(B19:B29)

NEW SKILL ▶ 11. Select cells A1 – H30 and set the AutoFormat feature to "List 2."
   Note: If "List 2" is not an option, select an alternate AutoFormat style to apply to the above cells.

12. Insert a header that shows:
    a. Left Section Activity 38-Student Name
    b. Center Section ABERCROMBIE AND FITCH 2
    c. Right Section Current Date
13. Insert a footer that shows:
    a. Center Section PAGE number
14. Display formulas in your spreadsheet by using <CTRL> + ` to check for accuracy.
15. Carefully proofread your work for accuracy.
16. Save the spreadsheet as ABERCROMBIE & FITCH 2.
17. Analyze the changes made to the data in the spreadsheet.
18. Set the Print Area to include all cells containing data in the spreadsheet.
19. Print Preview and adjust the Page Setup so that the spreadsheet fits on one page. Set the page orientation to landscape.
20. Print a copy of the spreadsheet if required by your instructor.

	A	B	C	D	E	F	G	H
1	**ABERCROMBIE & FITCH**							
2	**Markup Schedule November 2005**							
3								
4								
5		**ITEM**			**UNIT**	**SELLING**	$	%
6		**NUMBER**	**ITEM**	**STYLE**	**COST**	**PRICE**	MARKUP	MARKUP
7								
8	**Men's wear**	66147091	Polo	Salmon Lake	15.00	34.50		
9		68047979	Henleys	Caroga Lake	20.00	39.50		
10		67252066	Tees Short Sleeve Logo	Mount Colden	10.00	19.50		
11		68046404	Fleece	Roaring Brook	20.00	39.50		
12		73012342	Denim Jacket	Bull Point	60.00	79.50		
13		65014099	Sweater	Ridge Trail	20.00	39.50		
14		72024865	Jeans	Kilburn low rise boot	20.00	39.50		
15		71032968	Classic Pants	Woodfalls cargo	25.00	44.50		
16		70033081	Shorts	Bradshaw cargo	20.00	39.50		
17	Total Items							
18								
19	**Women's wear**	97170590	Message Tees	Beauty and Brains	6.00	15.50		
20		81367542	Tanks/Camis	Cecilia	5.00	12.50		
21		81373714	Knits	Danielle	15.00	24.50		
22		82050120	Pullover Fleece	Kylie velvet	20.00	39.50		
23		82048637	Track Jackets	Jaime	40.00	59.50		
24		80042350	Sweaters	Alyssa	30.00	49.50		
25		90014006	Denim Jackets	Tori	65.00	89.50		
26		90014048	Outerwear	Heather	75.00	128.00		
27		86045021	Jeans	Ashley super flare	20.00	39.50		
28		85094002	Active Pants	Jane stitch	15.00	34.50		
29		88033853	Denim Skirts	Cynthia	28.00	54.50		
30	Total Items							

Source: http://www.abercrombie.com/anf/lifestyles/html/homepage.html

ACTIVITY 39: MUSIC GENRES

New Skills Reinforced:

In this activity, you will practice how to:

1. import a text file into Excel.
2. use cell borders to highlight a cell's importance.

Activity Overview:

Allmusic.com, created in 1995, is one of the Web's best resources for all things music. It is a complete source of information including facts about an artist, details about an album, relational information about artists such as similar type artists, and finally, editorial commentary such as reviews and top picks. Internet users who are interested in any genre of music will find what they are looking for here. Nothing is left out, and the site can be depended on to provide an unbiased look at what's happening in music today.

The following activity illustrates how spreadsheets can be used to organize data, such as a list of music albums, from an external file.

Instructions:

1. Open a program that allows you to save a file as "Text" (.TXT) such as Notepad or Microsoft Word.
2. Type the data exactly as shown in Table 1-39. Use the <Enter> key after each line is keyed. Skip one line after the title "Music Genres."
3. Save the file as MUSIC GENRES.txt. Take note of where the file is saved so that it can be retrieved in step 5.
4. Create a NEW spreadsheet.
5. NEW SKILL ▶ Click on the "Data" menu and choose "Get External Data" then "Import Text File." Choose the MUSIC GENRES.txt file created in step 2.
   a. Set the original data type as DELIMITED.
   b. Use COMMA as the only delimiter.
   c. The data format for each column should be GENERAL.
   The data should now appear in the existing worksheet.

Note: Unless otherwise stated, the font should be set to Arial, the font size to 10 point.

6. Bold cell A1 and change the font size to 16 point.
7. NEW SKILL ▶ Format cells A3, B3, and C3 to display a double line border outside and inside of each cell. See Table 2-39 to see what your spreadsheet should look like.
8. Insert a header that shows:
   a. Left Section Activity 39-Student Name
   b. Center Section MUSIC GENRES
   c. Right Section Current Date
9. Insert a footer that shows:
   a. Center Section PAGE number
10. Carefully proofread your work for accuracy.
11. Save the spreadsheet as MUSIC GENRES.
12. Set the Print Area to include all cells containing data in the spreadsheet.
13. Print Preview and adjust the Page Setup so that the spreadsheet fits on one page.
14. Print a copy of the spreadsheet if required by your instructor.

ACTIVITY 39: MUSIC GENRES DATA SPREADSHEET

Table 1-39

Instructions: Type the data exactly as shown below using a program that allows you to save the file as a "text only" file (.TXT file extension). Save the file as MUSIC GENRES.txt.

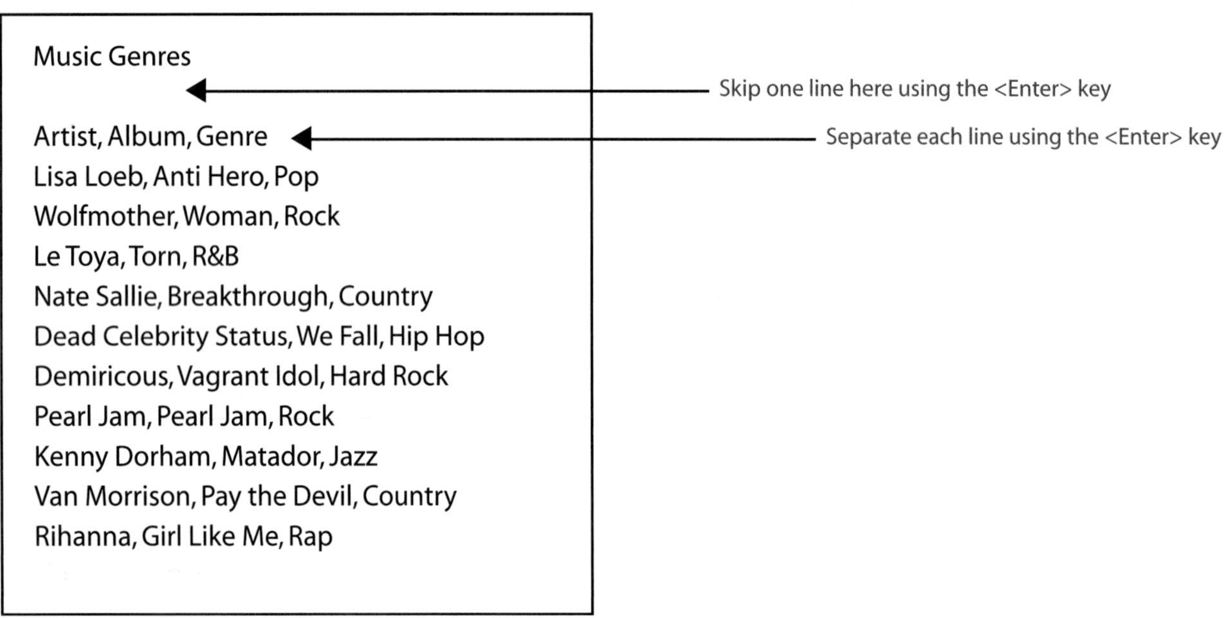

Music Genres

Skip one line here using the <Enter> key

Artist, Album, Genre
Lisa Loeb, Anti Hero, Pop
Wolfmother, Woman, Rock
Le Toya, Torn, R&B
Nate Sallie, Breakthrough, Country
Dead Celebrity Status, We Fall, Hip Hop
Demiricous, Vagrant Idol, Hard Rock
Pearl Jam, Pearl Jam, Rock
Kenny Dorham, Matador, Jazz
Van Morrison, Pay the Devil, Country
Rihanna, Girl Like Me, Rap

Separate each line using the <Enter> key

Table 2-39

Music Genres

Artist	Album	Genre
Lisa Loeb	Anti Hero	Pop
Wolfmother	Woman	Rock
Le Toya	Torn	R&B
Nate Sallie	Breakthrough	Country
Dead Celebrity Status	We Fall	Hip Hop
Demiricous	Vagrant Idol	Hard Rock
Pearl Jam	Pearl Jam	Rock
Kenny Dorham	Matador	Jazz
Van Morrison	Pay the Devil	Country
Rihanna	Girl Like Me	Rap

ACTIVITY 40: CHICAGO WHITE SOX® 2

New Skills Reinforced:

In this activity, you will practice how to:

1. print a spreadsheet with row and column headings.

Activity Overview:

The following activity illustrates how spreadsheets are used to list the Chicago White Sox® players statistics. This activity expands on the Chicago White Sox® spreadsheet created in Activity 14.

Instructions:

1. Open the file CHICAGO WHITE SOX previously created in Activity 14.
   Note: In this activity, you will not add any data to the spreadsheet. You will only be changing the spreadsheet's page setup to show row and column headings. Thus, there is no data spreadsheet provided.
2. Change the Activity # in cell A1 to Activity 40.
3. Set the Print Area to include all cells containing data in the spreadsheet.
4. **NEW SKILL** Print Preview and adjust the Page Setup so that the spreadsheet fits on one page. Set the page orientation to landscape, and the sheet to print gridlines and to show row and column headings. The column and row headings should appear in the Print Preview.
5. Save the spreadsheet as CHICAGO WHITE SOX 2.
6. Print a copy of the spreadsheet if required by your instructor.

ACTIVITY 41: YEARLY EARNINGS

New Skills Reinforced:

In this activity, you will practice how to:
1. freeze panes in a spreadsheet.

Activity Overview:

When you receive a paycheck, it is important to examine the "pay stub," an attachment that shows the total pay earned and any deductions such as taxes, social security, Medicare, and IRA's (Individual Retirement Accounts). The amount you earn before taxes and deductions are made to your paycheck is known as your "gross pay." The amount you actually are paid, or "take home," is known as your "net pay."

The following activity illustrates how spreadsheets can be used to calculate a person's weekly and annual gross and net pay. **Note:** In this activity, the employee is paid an hourly rate plus overtime. Overtime is calculated at time and one-half. Or, the hourly rate multiplied by 1.5. To view the headings near the top of a large spreadsheet while scrolling down, it is helpful to freeze the headings. This is known as "Freeze Panes." You will be applying this feature in this activity.

Instructions:

1. Create a NEW spreadsheet.

   Note: Unless otherwise stated, the font should be set to Arial, the font size to 10 point.
2. Type the data as shown. Type your name in cell A1.
3. Bold rows 1 – 5 and row 33.
4. Underline row 5.
5. Format the width of column A to 12.0 and left align.
6. Format cells A7 – A32 as dates showing mm/dd/yyyy.
7. Format the width of columns B and D to 10.0 and center align.
8. Format the width of column C to 10.0 and center align.
9. Format cells C7 – C32 as numbers displaying 2 decimal places.
10. Format the width of column E to 10.0 and center align.
11. Format the width of columns F – L to 10.0 and right align.
12. Format cells E7 – L33 as numbers displaying 2 decimal places.
13. **NEW SKILL** To make the column headings visible while scrolling down, apply Freeze Panes to the spreadsheet. To do this, place your mouse pointer on cell A6 and choose Window, Freeze Panes.
14. Compute the formulas for the first pay date as follows:
    a. OVERTIME RATE=HOURLY RATE * 1.5 -> In cell E7, type =C7*1.5
    b. GROSS PAY=(HOURS WORKED * HOURLY RATE) + (OVERTIME HOURS * OVERTIME RATE) -> In cell F7, type =(B7*C7)+(D7*E7)
    c. FEDERAL TAX=GROSS PAY * 15 % -> In cell G7, type =F7*15%
    d. SOCIAL SEC. TAX=GROSS PAY * 6.2 % -> In cell H7, type =F7*6.2%

e. MEDICARE TAX=GROSS PAY * 1.45 % -> In cell I7, type =F7*1.45%

f. STATE TAX=GROSS PAY * 4 % -> In cell J7, type =F7*4%

g. 401K PLAN=GROSS PAY * 10% -> In cell K7, type =F7*10%

h. NET PAY=GROSS PAY – Total Deductions -> In cell L7, type =F7-SUM(G7:K7)

15. Use the AutoFill feature to copy the formulas down for the remaining employees.
16. Enter formulas to compute the Totals for columns F – L.
17. Bold row 33.
18. Insert a header that shows:
    a. Left Section Activity 41-Student Name
    b. Center Section YEARLY EARNINGS
    c. Right Section Current Date
19. Insert a footer that shows:
    a. Center Section PAGE number
20. Display formulas in your spreadsheet by using <CTRL> + ` to check for accuracy.
21. Carefully proofread your work for accuracy.
22. Save the spreadsheet as YEARLY EARNINGS.
23. Analyze the changes made to the data in the spreadsheet.
24. Set the Print Area to include all cells containing data in the spreadsheet.
25. Print Preview and adjust the Page Setup so that the spreadsheet fits on one page. Set the page orientation to landscape.
26. Print a copy of the spreadsheet if required by your instructor.

ACTIVITY 41: YEARLY EARNINGS DATA SPREADSHEET

	A	B	C	D	E	F	G	H	I	J	K	L
1	STUDENT NAME											
2	2005 YEARLY EARNINGS											
3												
4		HOURS	HOURLY	OVERTIME	OVERTIME	GROSS	FEDERAL	SOCIAL	MEDICARE	STATE	401K	NET
5	PAY DATE	WORKED	RATE	HOURS	RATE	PAY	TAX	SEC. TAX	TAX	TAX	PLAN	PAY
6												
7	1/14/2005	75	13.00	0								
8	1/28/2005	80	13.00	3								
9	2/11/2005	80	13.00	4								
10	2/25/2005	76	13.00	0								
11	3/11/2005	74	13.00	0								
12	3/25/2005	78	13.00	0								
13	4/8/2005	73	13.00	0								
14	4/22/2005	70	13.00	0								
15	5/6/2005	78	13.00	0								
16	5/20/2005	71	13.00	0								
17	6/3/2005	80	13.00	1								
18	6/17/2005	74	13.00	0								
19	7/1/2005	79	13.00	0								
20	7/15/2005	80	13.50	2								
21	7/29/2005	76	13.50	0								
22	8/12/2005	80	13.50	3								
23	8/26/2005	80	13.50	4								
24	9/9/2005	77	13.50	0								
25	9/23/2005	70	13.50	0								
26	10/7/2005	73	13.50	0								
27	10/21/2005	75	13.50	0								
28	11/4/2005	72	13.50	0								
29	11/18/2005	75	13.50	0								
30	12/2/2005	80	13.50	2								
31	12/16/2005	80	13.50	7								
32	12/30/2005	80	13.50	8								
33	TOTALS											

ACTIVITY 42: TEEN CARS

New Skills Reinforced:

In this activity, you will practice how to:

1. insert WordArt in a spreadsheet.
2. edit and format WordArt.

Activity Overview:

One thing that every teenager looks forward to is obtaining a driver's license and driving a new car. Auto manufacturers have created lower-priced cars that make the dream of driving a reality for the teen market. Each year, edmunds.com, an informational Web site designed for car buyers, publishes its "Top 10 Cheap Cool Cars for Teens."

In this activity, you will be entering edmunds.com's picks for 2006 into a spreadsheet. You will enhance the appearance of the spreadsheet by using WordArt.

Instructions:

1. Create a NEW spreadsheet.

   Note: Unless otherwise stated, the font should be set to Arial, the font size to 10 point.
2. Type the data as shown. Do not insert the WordArt image shown until step 8.
3. Format the width of column A to 16.0 and left align.
4. Format the width of column B to 30.0 and left align.
5. Format the width of columns C and D to 16.0 and right align.
6. Format cells C9 – D18 as currency displaying 0 decimal places and the $ symbol.
7. Change the font size of cells A6 – D18 to 16 point.
8. **NEW SKILL** Insert a WordArt image similar to the one shown in the Activity 42 Data Spreadsheet. Edit the WordArt text to read "Top 10 Cheap Cool Cars for Teens for 2006" and change the font size to 24. Select a font of your choice. Place the WordArt image so it is centered above the data entered in columns A – D.
9. Insert a header that shows:
   a. Left Section — Activity 42-Student Name
   b. Center Section — TEEN CARS
   c. Right Section — Current Date
10. Insert a footer that shows:
    a. Center Section — PAGE number
11. Carefully proofread your work for accuracy.
12. Save the spreadsheet as TEEN CARS.
13. Analyze the changes made to the data in the spreadsheet.
14. Set the Print Area to include all cells containing data in the spreadsheet.
15. Print Preview and adjust the Page Setup so that the spreadsheet fits on one page.
16. Print a copy of the spreadsheet if required by your instructor.

ACTIVITY 42: TEEN CARS DATA SPREADSHEET

	A	B	C	D
1	Top 10 Cheap Cool Cars for Teens for 2006			
2				
3				
4				
5				
6			MSRP	MSRP
7	Year	Make	Low	High
8				
9	2006	Honda Civic	14360	21940
10	2006	Mazda 3	13710	19165
11	2006	Scion tC	16300	17100
12	2006	Scion xB	14030	14830
13	2007	Honda Fit	13850	15970
14	2006	Ford Mustang	19115	26320
15	2006	Volkswagen Jetta	17900	24865
16	2006	Mitsubishi Eclipse	17900	24865
17	2007	Nissan Versa	12000	16000
18	2006	Pontiac Vibe	15260	19250

ACTIVITY 43: TV SHOW STANDINGS

New Skills Reinforced:

In this activity, you will practice how to:

1. insert a line from the drawing toolbar.

Activity Overview:

Nielsen Ratings® is a system developed by Neilsen Media Research®, a media market research company that tracks the audience size for television, radio, and newspapers. Each week, Neilsen Ratings® are published to rank television program viewership. This information helps networks to see how well certain shows are doing and gives value to a show's advertising potential. Statistics are gathered either by households that maintain a personal diary of the shows they watch or by a small computer connected to each television in a household that tracks and submits data to Neilsen Media Research®. The households surveyed or tracked encompass a wide variety of demographics. The system has been around since its development in the 1960s.

The following activity illustrates how spreadsheets can be used to track the results of a particular week's top-rated television shows. In this activity, you will be using the drawing toolbar to enhance the appearance of a spreadsheet.

Instructions:

1. Create a NEW spreadsheet.

   Note: Unless otherwise stated, the font should be set to Arial, the font size to 10 point.
2. Type the data as shown.
3. Change the font size of cell A1 to 18 point.
4. Change the font size of cell A2 to 16 point.
5. Format the height of row 4 to 48.0.
6. Use the AutoFill feature to complete the numbering sequence in cells A5 – A24 for the Rankings in column A.
7. Format the width of column A to 7.0 and left align.
8. Format the width of column B to 30.0 and left align.
9. Format the width of columns C and D to 10.0 and center align.
10. Format the width of column E to 15.0 and center align.
11. Format cells E5 – E24 as time showing h:mm pm.
12. Format the width of columns F and G to 8.0 and right align.
13. Format cells F5 – G24 as numbers displaying 1 decimal place.
14. Format the width of column H to 15.0 and right align.
15. Format cells H5 – H24 as numbers displaying 0 decimals using a comma separator.
16. **NEW SKILL** From the Draw Toolbar, insert a horizontal line in the spreadsheet. Change the line weight to 1.5 pts. Place the line between rows 4 and 5. Resize the line so it stretches across columns A – H.

17. Insert a header that shows:
    a. Left Section Activity 43-Student Name
    b. Center Section TV SHOW STANDINGS
    c. Right Section Current Date
18. Insert a footer that shows:
    a. Center Section PAGE number
19. Carefully proofread your work for accuracy.
20. Save the spreadsheet as TV SHOW STANDINGS.
21. Analyze the changes made to the data in the spreadsheet.
22. Set the Print Area to include all cells containing data in the spreadsheet.
23. Print Preview and adjust the Page Setup so that the spreadsheet fits on one page.
24. Print a copy of the spreadsheet if required by your instructor.

ACTIVITY 43: TV SHOW STANDINGS DATA SPREADSHEET

	A	B	C	D	E	F	G	H
1	Nielsen Media Research Top 20							
2	Week of March 20-26, 2006							
3								
4	Rank	Program Name	Network	Day	Time	Rating	Share	Households
5	1	American Idol - Tuesday	FOX	Tue	8:00 PM	19.2	28	21157000
6	2	American Idol - Wednesday	FOX	Wed	9:00 PM	15.9	24	17575000
7		Desperate Housewives	ABC	Sun	9:00 PM	13.5	20	12910000
8		CSI:Miami	CBS	Mon	10:00 PM	13	21	14333000
9		60 Minutes	CBS	Sun	7:39 PM	11	17	12077000
10		Two and a Half Men	CBS	Mon	9:00 PM	10.5	15	10800000
11		Deal or No Deal	NBC	Mon	8:00 PM	9.8	15	10800000
12		The Unit	CBS	Tue	9:00 PM	9.8	14	10770000
13		Grey's Anatomy	ABC	Sun	10:01 PM	9.7	16	10679000
14		Lost	ABC	Wed	9:00 PM	9.7	14	10672000
15		Old Christine	CBS	Mon	9:30 PM	9.7	14	10699000
16		Unanimous	FOX	Wed	9:30 PM	9.5	14	10434000
17		Cold Case	CBS	Sun	8:39 PM	9.4	14	10310000
18		Law and Order: SVU	NBC	Tue	10:00 PM	9.2	15	10149000
19		CSI: NY	CBS	Wed	10:00 PM	9.1	15	10055000
20		E.R.	NBC	Thu	9:59 PM	9	15	9963000
21		Deal or No Deal	NBC	Wed	8:00 PM	8.9	14	9806000
22		CBS NCAA Post	CBS	Sun	7:31 PM	8.5	15	9353000
23		24	FOX	Mon	9:00 PM	8.3	12	9160000
24		American Inventor	ABC	Thu	9:00 PM	8	12	8783000

Source: http://tv.yahoo.com/nielsen/

ACTIVITY 44: STUDENT TRAVEL

New Skills Reinforced:

In this activity, you will practice how to:
1. format cells as accounting.
2. apply borders to a cell range.

Activity Overview:

Many students love to travel but hate the high prices of airfare. However, many discounts are available for the student traveler. Besides buying student-discounted railway passes and staying at youth hotels, students also have access to lower-priced airline tickets. The trick is to know where to shop and be flexible about where you want to go. Many Internet travel agents require that students sign up for newsletters and email alerts, but the hassle may be worth the money one can save on travel.

The following activity illustrates how spreadsheets can be used to list student-discounted airfares. In this activity, you will format a range of numbers in cells as Accounting.

Instructions:

1. Create a NEW spreadsheet.

   Note: Unless otherwise stated, the font should be set to Arial, the font size to 10 point.
2. Type the data as shown.
3. Change the font size of cell A1 to 16 point.
4. Format the width of column A to 20.0, column B to 12.0, and column C to 16.0.
5. Format the height of row 3 to 48.0 and bold the row.
6. NEW SKILL ▶ Format cells A3 – C3 with a thick border outline.
7. NEW SKILL ▶ Format column C as accounting displaying 2 decimal places and the $ symbol.
8. Insert a header that shows:
   a. Left Section — Activity 44-Student Name
   b. Center Section — STUDENT TRAVEL
   c. Right Section — Current Date
9. Insert a footer that shows:
   a. Center Section — PAGE number
10. Carefully proofread your work for accuracy.
11. Save the spreadsheet as STUDENT TRAVEL.
12. Analyze the changes made to the data in the spreadsheet.
13. Set the Print Area to include all cells containing data in the spreadsheet.
14. Print Preview and adjust the Page Setup so that the spreadsheet fits on one page.
15. Print a copy of the spreadsheet if required by your instructor.

ACTIVITY 44: STUDENT TRAVEL DATA SPREADSHEET

	A	B	C
1	Sample Student Airfares		
2			
3	Departing	Arriving	Round Trip Fare
4	San Francisco	Los Angeles	117
5	Memphis	Chicago	151
6	Boston	Indianapolis	172
7	Washington	Dallas	193
8	New York	London	203
9	Detroit	Denver	207
10	New York	Johannesburg	958
11	Philadelphia	Brussels	340
12	Boston	Paris	376
13	Washington	Prague	399
14	New York	Milan	408
15	Los Angeles	Berlin	513
16	Detroit	Amsterdam	598

ACTIVITY 45: AMERICAN IDOL®

New Skills Reinforced:

In this activity, you will practice how to:
1. create a pie chart.
2. enhance charts by changing colors and font sizes.

Activity Overview:

American Idol® has truly become one of America's biggest and most watched television shows. With its debut in the summer of 2002, this show, based on Britain's Pop Idol, became an instant success. Hosted by Ryan Seacrest, the Dick Clark of our day, American Idol® grows bigger and bigger each season. The show's three judges, Simon Cowell, Paula Abdul, and Randy Jackson have become household names, along with the winning contestants from each season.

The authors of this book surveyed 24 American Idol® viewers and asked who their favorite American Idol® singer was. The following activity illustrates how spreadsheets can be used to create a pie chart that illustrates this distribution.

Instructions:

1. Create a NEW spreadsheet.

   Note: Unless otherwise stated, the font should be set to Arial, the font size to 10 point.
2. Type the data as shown.
3. Change the font size of cell A1 to 16 point.
4. Format the width of column A to 26.0 and left align.
5. Format the width of column B to 22.0 and center align.
6. Bold rows 1 and 3.
7. **NEW SKILL** Create a pie chart as follows:
   a. Select cells A1– B8.
   b. Using the Chart Wizard, select Pie for the Chart type. The Chart sub-type should be Pie.
   c. Set the chart to Series in Columns.
   d. Enter the chart title as "AMERICAN IDOL FAVORITES."
   e. Display the legend to the right of the pie chart.
   f. Show no data labels.
   g. Save the chart as a new sheet. Name the new sheet AMERICAN IDOL CHART.
8. **NEW SKILL** Format the Chart Area with a background color of peach.
9. **NEW SKILL** Format the colors of each piece of the pie chart as follows:
   a. Kelly Clarkson -> purple
   b. Reuben Studdard -> green
   c. Clay Aiken -> yellow
   d. Fantasia Barrino -> turquoise
   e. Carrie Underwood -> pink

NEW SKILL

NEW SKILL

10. Format the chart's legend background color to light blue and change the font size to 16 point.
11. Format the chart's title to blue and change the font size to 24 point and bold.
12. When formatted, your chart should look similar to the one provided in Figure 1-45.
13. Insert a header for both the spreadsheet and the chart that shows:
    a. Left Section Activity 45-Student Name
    b. Center Section AMERICAN IDOL
    c. Right Section Current Date
14. Insert a footer that shows:
    a. Center Section PAGE number
15. Carefully proofread your work for accuracy.
16. Analyze the changes made to the data in the spreadsheet.
17. Save the spreadsheet as AMERICAN IDOL.
18. Print Preview and adjust the Page Setup so that the spreadsheet and the chart each fit on one page. Set the page orientation to landscape for the chart.
19. Print a copy of the spreadsheet and chart if required by your instructor.

ACTIVITY 45: AMERICAN IDOL® DATA SPREADSHEET

	A	B	C
1	AMERICAN IDOL		
2			
3	CONTESTANT	VOTES FOR FAVORITE	
4	Kelly Clarkson	7	
5	Reuben Studdard	5	
6	Clay Aiken	3	
7	Fantasia Barrino	5	
8	Carrie Underwood	4	

Figure 1-45

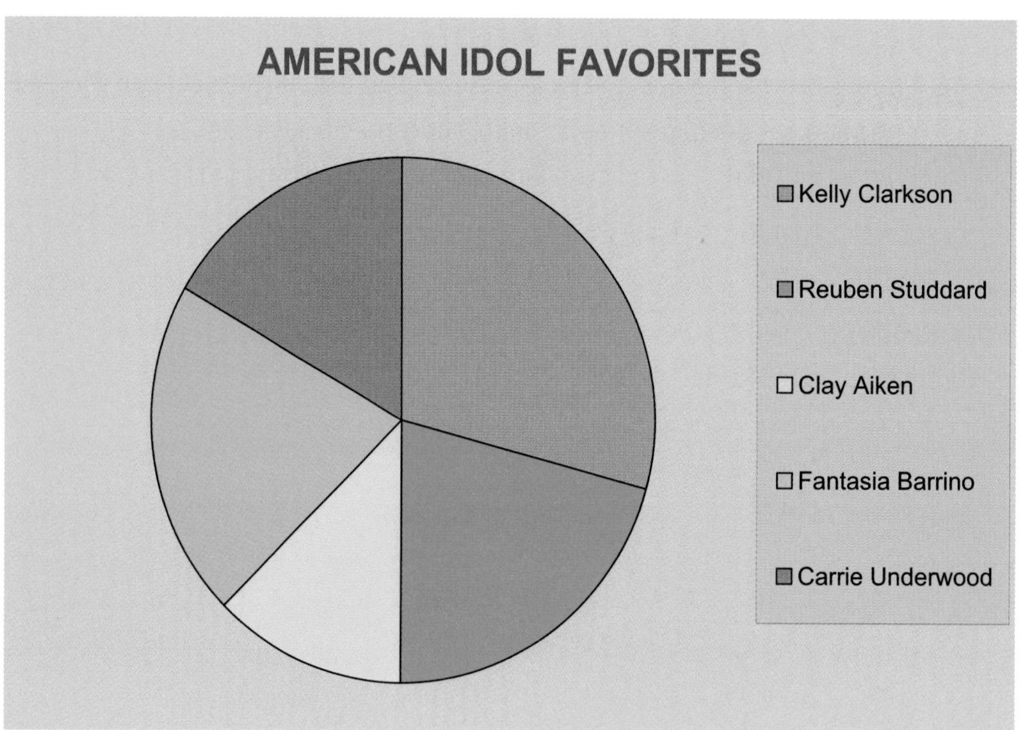

ACTIVITY 46: ITUNES®

New Skills Reinforced:

In this activity, you will practice how to:

1. create a column chart.

Activity Overview:

The existence of iTunes® has made it easy for anyone with a computer and an Internet connection to create and organize their own music and video library. Songs and music videos can be downloaded from Apple's® iTunes® Web site (*www.itunes.com*) quickly and easily. Users can share music with other users, create playlists, and take their music collections with them wherever they want on an iPod®. The popularity of iTunes® is forecasted to continue to grow.

The following activity illustrates how spreadsheets can be used to create a bar graph to analyze the frequency of popular iTunes® downloaded.

Instructions:

1. Create a NEW spreadsheet.
   Note: Unless otherwise stated, the font should be set to Arial, the font size to 10 point.
2. Type the data as shown.
3. Change the font size in cell A1 to 16 point and bold the cell.
4. Format the width of column A to 36.0 and left align.
5. Format the width of column B to 14.0 and center align.
6. Bold row 3.
7. NEW SKILL ▶ Create a column chart as follows:
   a. Select cells A3 – B13.
   b. Using the Chart Wizard, select Column for the Chart type and Clustered Column for the Chart sub-type.
   c. Set the chart to Series in Columns.
   d. Enter the chart title as "MOST POPULAR iTUNES DOWNLOADED," the title for category (X) axis as "SONG, ARTIST" and the title for value (Y) axis as "FREQUENCY."
   e. Display the legend to the right of the chart.
   f. Show no data labels.
   g. Save the chart as a new sheet. Name the new sheet iTUNES CHART.
8. Format the style and colors of the chart as follows:
   a. Change the background color of the Chart Area to turquoise.
   b. Change the background color of the Plot Area to yellow.
   c. Change the colors of the bars to purple.
   d. Format the chart title and axis titles to font size 12 point and bold.
   e. Change the text alignment of the song titles to 90 degrees.
   f. Change the major unit of the frequency numbers to 2000 and the minor unit to 500.

9. When formatted, your chart should look similar to the one provided in Figure 1-46.
10. Insert a header for both the spreadsheet and the chart that shows:
    a. Left Section Activity 46-Student Name
    b. Center Section iTUNES
    c. Right Section Current Date
11. Insert a footer for both the chart and spreadsheet that shows:
    a. Center Section PAGE number
12. Carefully proofread your work for accuracy.
13. Save the spreadsheet as iTUNES.
14. Analyze the changes made to the data in the spreadsheet.
15. Print Preview and adjust the Page Setup so that the spreadsheet and the chart each fit on one page. Set the page orientation to landscape for the chart.
16. Print a copy of the spreadsheet and chart if required by your instructor.

	A	B
1	MOST POPULAR iTUNES DOWNLOADED	
2		
3	SONG, ARTIST	FREQUENCY
4	Hung Up, Madonna	23,548
5	Run It!, Chris Brown	20,874
6	My Humps, Black Eyed Peas	17,311
7	Photograph, Nickelback	15,143
8	Stickwitu, The Pussycat Dolls	14,924
9	Laffy Taffy, D4L	13,882
10	Dance, Dance, Fall Out Boy	13,233
11	Gold Digger, Kanye West	12,716
12	Sugar, We're Going Down, Fall Out Boy	11,533
13	There It Go!, Juelz Santana	10,135

Figure 1-46

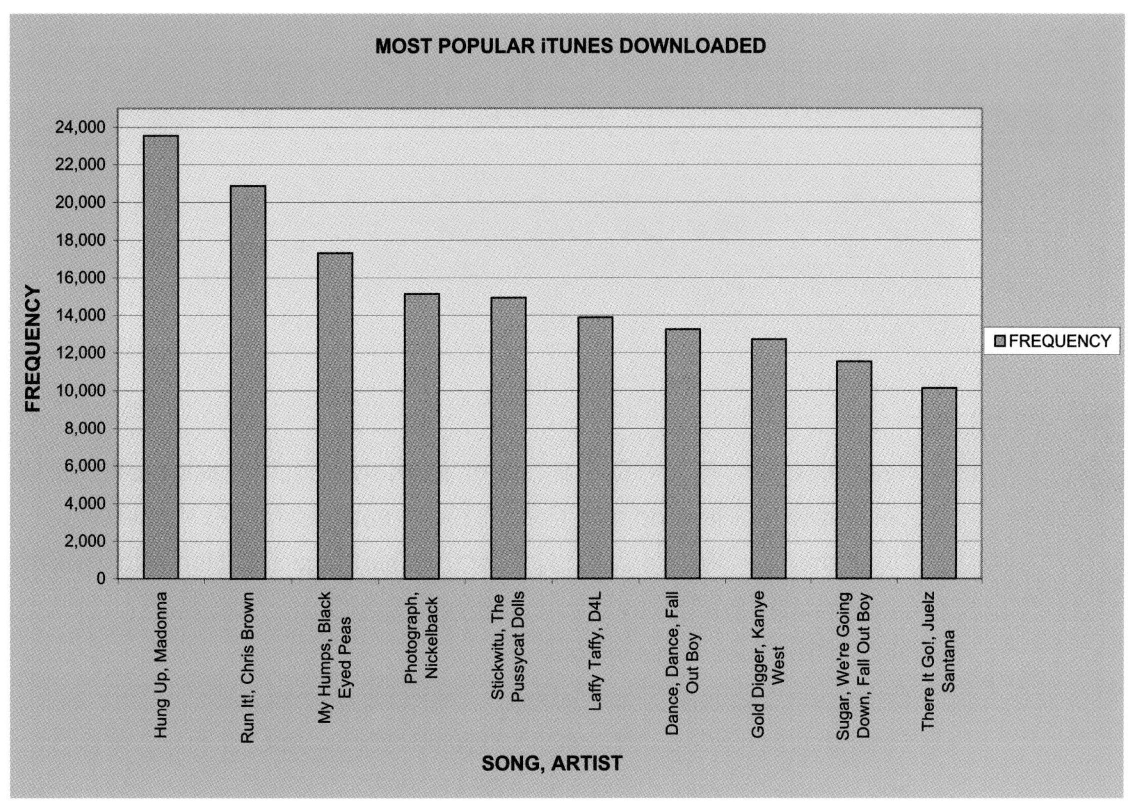

ACTIVITY 47: X GAMES®

New Skills Reinforced:

In this activity, you will practice how to:
1. create a line chart.
2. select cells using multiple ranges.
3. use the Fill Effects feature in a chart.

Activity Overview:

With the debut of the X Games® in 1995, extreme sports became visible and more main stream. Sports such as BMX, skateboarding, wakeboarding, snowboarding, and surfing finally received recognition as "real sports." Athletes that perform extreme sports are now just as famous as baseball, football, and basketball stars. Sports enthusiasts and spectators alike seem to enjoy the thrill and action involved in these sports. Young children now aspire to be just like the thrill-seekers that they watch during the X Games®.

The following activity illustrates how spreadsheets can be used to graph the spectator attendance at X Games® over the years.

Instructions:

1. Create a NEW spreadsheet.

   Note: Unless otherwise stated, the font should be set to Arial, the font size to 10 point.
2. Type the data as shown.
3. Bold cell A1 and change the font size to 16 point.
4. Bold and underline row 3.
5. Format column widths and alignments as follows:
   a. Column A to 8.0 and left align.
   b. Column B to 16.0 and left align.
   c. Column C to 22.0 and left align.
   d. Column D to 24.0 and center align.

NEW SKILL ▶ 6. Create a line chart as follows:

NEW SKILL ▶ a. Select cells A3 – A9 and D3 – D9 simultaneously. To do this, select cells A3 – D9, then, hold down <CTRL> and select cells D3 – D9. Both cell ranges should be selected.

   b. Using the Chart Wizard, select Line for the Chart type and "Line with markers displayed at each data value" for the Chart sub-type.
   c. Set the line chart Series in Columns.
   d. Define the Category (X) axis labels by selecting cells A4 – A9.
   e. Enter the chart title as "XGAMES ATTENDANCE," the title for category (X) axis as "YEAR," and the title for value (Y) axis as "# OF PEOPLE."
   f. Display the legend to the right of the chart.
   g. Show no data labels.
   h. Save the chart as a new sheet. Name the new sheet XGAMES CHART.

NEW SKILL

7. Format the style and colors in the chart as follows:
   a. Change the background color of the Chart Area using the Fill Effects feature. Choose a Gradient effect with two colors. Set Color 1 to blue and color 2 to light pink with horizontal shading style.
   b. Change the background color of the Plot Area to peach.
   c. Change the font size of the title in the chart to 20 point.
   d. Change the font size of the X and Y axis titles to 14 point.
8. Change the text alignment of the YEARS to 90 degrees.
9. When formatted, your chart should look similar to the one provided in Figure 1-47.
10. Insert a header for both the spreadsheet and the chart that shows:
    a. Left Section — Activity 47-Student Name
    b. Center Section — XGAMES
    c. Right Section — Current Date
11. Insert a footer that shows:
    a. Center Section — PAGE number
12. Carefully proofread your work for accuracy.
13. Save the spreadsheet as XGAMES.
14. Analyze the changes made to the data in the spreadsheet.
15. Print Preview and adjust the Page Setup so that the spreadsheet and the chart each fit on one page. Set the page orientation to landscape for the chart.
16. Print a copy of the spreadsheet and the chart if required by your instructor.

ACTIVITY 47: X GAMES® DATA SPREADSHEET

	A	B	C	D
1	History of the X Games			
2				
3	Year	Number	Location	# of People in Attendance
4	1995	X Games One	Providence & Newport, RI	198000
5	1996	X Games Two	Newport, RI	200000
6	1997	X Games Three	San Diego, CA	221200
7	1998	X Games Four	San Diego, CA	233000
8	1999	X Games Five	San Francisco, CA	275000
9	2001	X Games Seven	Philadelphia, PA	235000
10				
11	Data not available for the years 2000, 2002, 2003, 2004, 2005, 2006.			

Source: http://en.wikipedia.org/wiki/X_Games#X_Games_Sports

Figure 1-47

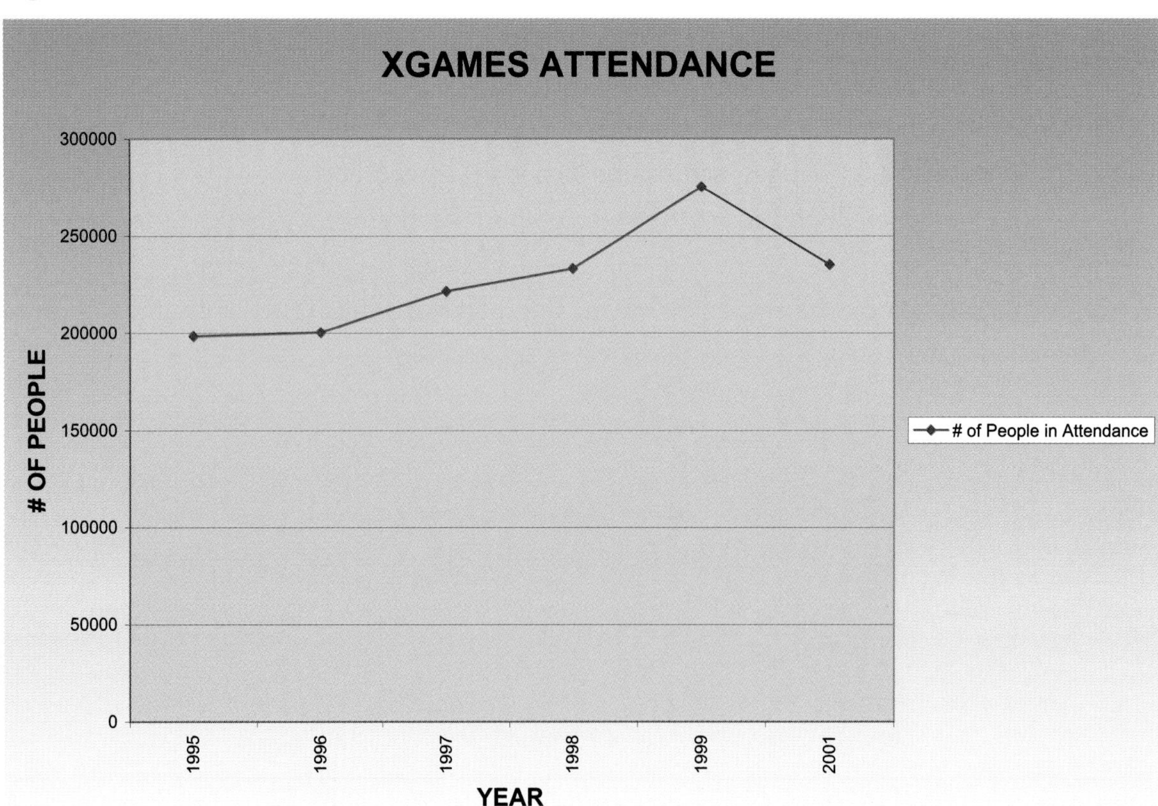

ACTIVITY 48: MTV®

New Skills Reinforced:

In this activity, you will practice how to:
1. create a bar chart.
2. align text in a chart.

Activity Overview:

In 1997, MTV® began what has now become a top-rated video show. Total Request Live, or TRL as it is more popularly known, airs daily on MTV® and highlights the day's most requested videos before a live audience. Registered members of MTV.com® can cast one vote per day for their favorite video. Each afternoon, TRL showcases the top 10 videos along with live performances and celebrity interviews. The show has a loyal following and is part of today's pop culture. Since videos may dominate the countdown for some time, the show has adopted a retirement program for all videos that stay on the countdown for 50 days.

The following activity illustrates how spreadsheets can be used to graphically compare the number of weeks a music video stayed at number one on MTV's® Total Request Live.

Instructions:

1. Create a NEW spreadsheet.
   Note: Unless otherwise stated, the font should be set to Arial, the font size to 10 point.
2. Type the data as shown.
3. Bold cell A1 and change the font size to 16 point.
4. Bold rows 1, 2, and 4.
5. Left align cells A4 – D20.
6. Format the width of columns A – C to 22.0.
7. Format the width of column D to 12.0.

NEW SKILL ▶

8. Create a bar chart as follows:
   a. Select cells B4 – B20 and D4 – D20 simultaneously. To do this, select cells B4 – B20 then, hold down <CTRL> and select cells D4 – D20. Both cell ranges should be selected.
   b. Using the Chart Wizard, select Bar for the Chart type and Clustered Bar for the Chart sub-type.
   c. Set the bar chart to Series in Columns.
   d. Enter the chart title as "WEEKS AT #1," the title for category (X) axis as "SONG," and the title for value (Y) axis as "# OF WEEKS."
   e. Display the legend to the right of the chart.
   f. Show no data labels.
   g. Save chart as a new sheet. Name the new sheet as MTV CHART.

9. Format the style of the chart as follows:
    a. Change the font size of the song titles to 8 point.
    b. Change the font size of the title to 16 point and bold.
    c. Change the text alignment of the songs to 45 degrees. NEW SKILL
10. When formatted, your chart should look similar to the one provided in Figure 1-48.
11. Insert a header for both the spreadsheet and the chart that shows:
    a. Left Section Activity 48-Student Name
    b. Center Section MTV
    c. Right Section Current Date
12. Insert a footer that shows:
    a. Center Section PAGE number
13. Carefully proofread your work for accuracy.
14. Save the spreadsheet as MTV.
15. Analyze the changes made to the data in the spreadsheet.
16. Print Preview and adjust the Page Setup so that the spreadsheet and the chart each fit on one page. Set the page orientation to landscape for the chart.
17. Print a copy of the spreadsheet and chart if required by your instructor.

ACTIVITY 48: MTV® DATA SPREADSHEET

	A	B	C	D
1	MTV Total Request Live			
2	Retired Videos			
3				
4	Artist	Song	Label	Weeks at #1
5	Madonna	Hung Up	Warner Bros.	20
6	Mariah Carey	Don't Forget About Us	Island	25
7	Hilary Duff	Wake Up	Hollywood Records	15
8	Gwen Stefani	Hollaback Girl	Interscope	50
9	Simple Plan	Untitled	Lava	23
10	Outkast	Roses	LaFace	44
11	D12	My Band	Shady/Interscope Records	42
12	Beyonce	Naughty Girl	Columbia Records	38
13	Britney Spears	Everytime	Jive	39
14	Britney Spears	Toxic	Jive	43
15	Hilary Duff	So Yesterday	Hollywood Records	40
16	Good Charlotte	Hold On	Daylight/Epic Records	35
17	Clay Aiken	The Way	RCA	30
18	JoJo	Leave (Get Out)	Da Family	41
19	Blink 182	Feeling This	Geffen Records	26
20	Clay Aiken	Invisible	RCA	28

Source: MTV.com

Figure 1-48

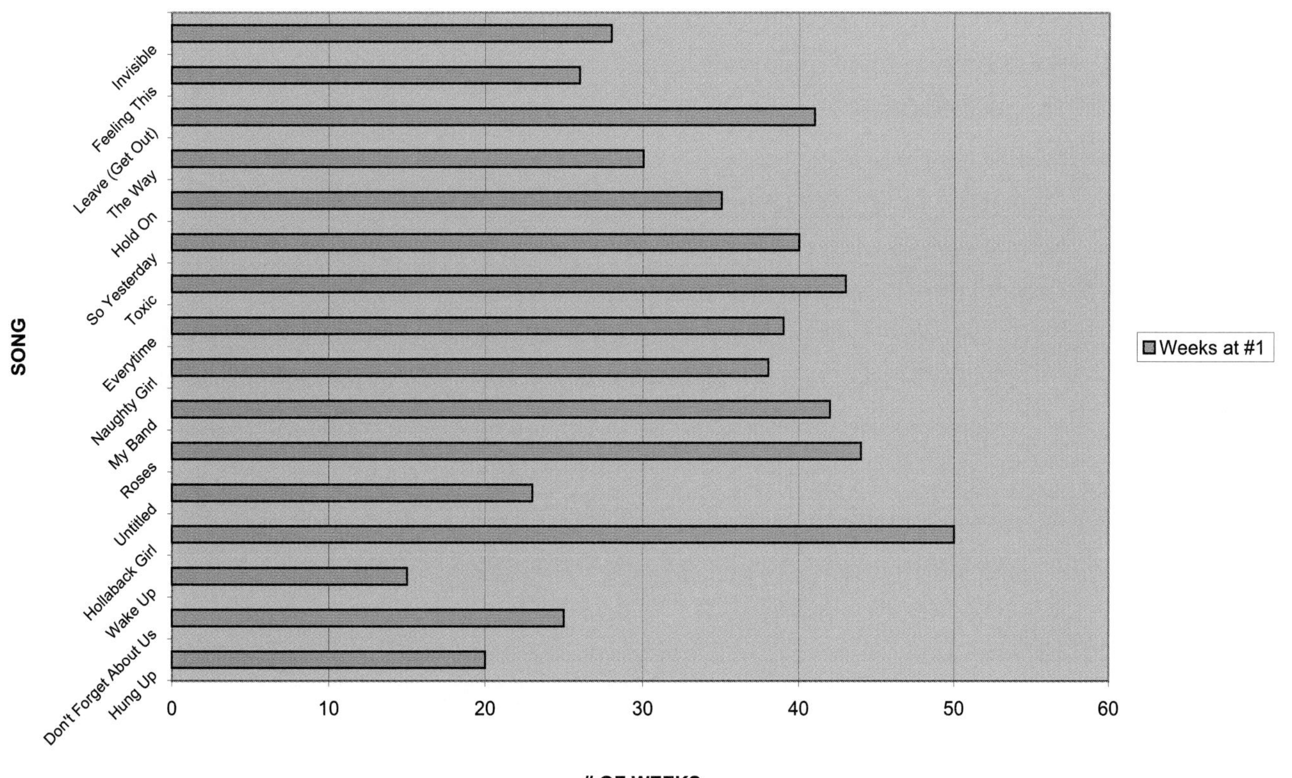

ACTIVITY 49: RAISE

New Skills Reinforced:

In this activity, you will practice how to:

1. use conditions in formulas to determine a desired result.

Activity Overview:

The Castleton Company is changing its procedures on salary raises. Instead of everyone getting the same raise, management has decided to base raises on the condition of number of years of service to the company. Employees who have been with the company five years or more will receive a 4.5 percent raise. All other employees will receive a 3 percent raise.

The following activity illustrates how spreadsheets can be used to calculate the raise percent, actual raises, bonuses, and determine each employee's salary for 2006.

Instructions:

1. Create a NEW spreadsheet.

   Note: Unless otherwise stated, the font should be set to Arial, the font size to 10 point.
2. Type the data as shown.
3. Bold rows 1 – 6 and row 21.
4. Format the width of columns A and B to 15.0 and left align.
5. Format the width of column C to 13.0 and center align.
6. Format the width of columns D, F, and G to 13.0 and right align.
7. Format cells D8 – D21 and cells F8 – G21 as currency displaying 2 decimal places and the $ symbol.
8. Format the width of column E to 13.0 and center align
9. Format cells E8 – E20 as percentages displaying 2 decimal places.
10. Compute the formulas for the first employee as follows:

    NEW SKILL

    a. In column E, % INCREASE, a conditional formula is required to determine if each employee's YEARS OF SERVICE is greater than or equal to 5 years. If the condition is true, the employee receives a 4.5% increase to his/her 2005 SALARY. If the condition is false, the employee receives a 3% increase to his/her 2005 SALARY. The conditional formula for the first employee is given below. In cell E8, type =IF(C8>=5,4.5%,3%)
    b. 2006 RAISE=2005 SALARY*% INCREASE -> In cell F8, type =D8*E8
    c. 2006 SALARY=2005 SALARY+2006 RAISE -> In cell G8, type =D8+F8
11. Use the AutoFill feature to copy the formulas down for the remaining employees.
12. Enter formulas to compute the totals for columns D, F, and G.

13. Insert a header that shows:
    a. Left Section Activity 49-Student Name
    b. Center Section RAISE
    c. Right Section Current Date
14. Insert a footer that shows:
    a. Center Section PAGE number
15. Display formulas in your spreadsheet by using <CTRL> + ` to check for accuracy.
16. Carefully proofread your work for accuracy.
17. Save the spreadsheet as RAISE.
18. Analyze the changes made to the data in the spreadsheet.
19. Set the Print Area to include all cells containing data in the spreadsheet.
20. Print Preview and adjust the Page Setup so that the spreadsheet fits on one page.
21. Print a copy of the spreadsheet if required by your instructor.

ACTIVITY 49: RAISE DATA SPREADSHEET

	A	B	C	D	E	F	G
1	CASTLETON INC.						
2	SCHEDULE OF RAISES						
3	EFFECTIVE DATE: 1/1/2006						
4							
5			YEARS OF	2005	%	2006	2006
6	LAST	FIRST	SERVICE	SALARY	INCREASE	RAISE	SALARY
7							
8	Acuin	Rita	16	49000			
9	Anthony	Thomas	11	35000			
10	Autovino	Sandy	5	17500			
11	Baptiste	Janice	3	20000			
12	Becknel	Carlos	15	23000			
13	Brothers	Jessica	4	27000			
14	Carrubba	Thomas	8	30000			
15	Chinnici	Virginia	9	35000			
16	Cleland	Rochelle	2	27000			
17	Depalma	Antonella	10	41500			
18	Dickerman	Gloria	3	27000			
19	Doyle	Samantha	11	43000			
20	Goldstein	Lane	15	55000			
21	TOTALS						

ACTIVITY 50: TEACHER'S GRADE BOOK

New Skills Reinforced:

In this activity, you will practice how to:
1. use the Median and Mode functions.
2. use multiple conditions in formulas to determine a desired result.

Activity Overview:

Assume that your computer teacher has asked you for help in setting up a spreadsheet to organize and calculate grades. The students have handed in three homework assignments and have taken four tests so far this semester.

In this activity, you will create a spreadsheet that calculates student's averages, determines whether a student passes or fails, and determines the letter grade students receive based on a conditional statement. For a student to PASS, his or her numerical average must be greater than or equal to 59.50. To determine the letter grade for each student, use the chart provided below.

Numerical Grade	Letter Grade Equivalent
Greater than or equal to 89.50	A
Greater than or equal to 79.50	B
Greater than or equal to 69.50	C
Greater than or equal to 59.50	D
Less than 59.50	F

In addition to using previously practiced skills, you will be using the MODE and MEDIAN functions. Each of these functions is defined below with respect to what each function yields in this activity.

MODE Calculates the most frequently achieved numerical grade for each assignment or test.
MEDIAN Calculates the numerical grade that falls in the middle of each assignment or test.

Instructions:

1. Create a NEW spreadsheet.

   Note: Unless otherwise stated, the font should be set to Arial, the font size to 10 point.
2. Type the data as shown.
3. Bold cell A1 and row 2.
4. Bold and underline row 3.
5. Format the width of columns A and B to 14.0 and left align.
6. Format the width of columns C – K to 8.0, column L to 10.0, and column M to 8.0.
7. Center align columns C – M.
8. Bold rows 41 – 45.
9. Format cells C5 – K45 as numbers displaying 0 decimal places.

10. Input the formulas for the first student as follows:
    a. In cell F5, the HW AVG (Homework Average), type =AVERAGE(C5:E5)
    b. In cell K5, the NUM. AVG (Numerical Average), type =AVERAGE(F5:J5)
    c. In cell L5, PASS/FAIL, type =IF(K5>=59.5,"PASS","FAIL")
    d. **NEW SKILL** In cell M5, the LETTER GRADE, type
    =IF(K5>=89.5,"A",IF(K5>=79.5,"B",IF(K5>=69.5,"C",IF(K5>=59.5,"D",IF(K5<59.5,"F")))))
11. Use the AutoFill feature to copy the formulas down for the remaining students.
12. Input the formulas for the AVERAGE, MAXIMUM, MINIMUM, MODE, and MEDIAN functions as follows:
    a. In cell C41, the AVERAGE, type =AVERAGE(C5:C39)
    b. In cell C42, the MAXIMUM, type =MAX(C5:C39)
    c. In cell C43, the MINIMUM, type =MIN(C5:C39)
    d. **NEW SKILL** In cell C44, the MODE, type =MODE(C5:C39)
    e. **NEW SKILL** In cell C45, the MEDIAN, type =MEDIAN(C5:C39)
13. Use the AutoFill feature to copy the formulas across to column K for the remaining homeworks (HW) and TESTS.
14. Insert a header that shows:
    a. Left Section Activity 50-Student Name
    b. Center Section TEACHER'S GRADE BOOK
    c. Right Section Current Date
15. Insert a footer that shows:
    a. Center Section PAGE number
16. Display formulas in your spreadsheet by using <CTRL> + ` to check for accuracy.
17. Carefully proofread your work for accuracy.
18. Save the spreadsheet as TEACHER'S GRADE BOOK.
19. Analyze the changes made to the data in the spreadsheet.
20. Set the Print Area to include all cells containing data in the spreadsheet.
21. Print Preview and adjust the Page Setup so that the spreadsheet fits on one page. Set the page orientation to landscape.
22. Print a copy of the spreadsheet if required by your instructor.

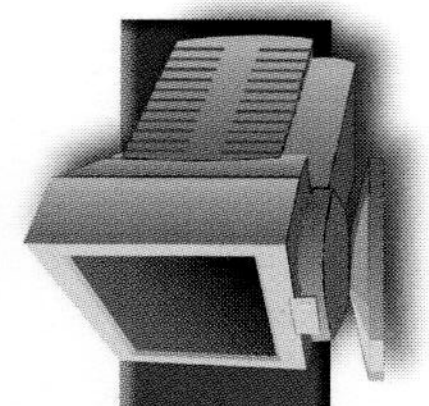

	A	B	C	D	E	F	G	H	I	J	K	L	M
1	MY TEACHER'S GRADE BOOK												
2						HW					NUM.		LETTER
3	LAST	FIRST	HW 1	HW 2	HW 3	AVG	TEST 1	TEST 2	TEST 3	TEST 4	AVG	PASS/FAIL	GRADE
4													
5	Allen	Casida	75	0	80		85	90	83	78			
6	Begum	Marvin	75	70	0		55	87	49	38			
7	Caines	Kevin	75	75	80		49	65	78	65			
8	Campbell	Jefferson	85	90	90		97	87	85	91			
9	Cheung	Alex	75	80	85		100	95	85	90			
10	Chu	Daisy	75	80	85		70	65	64	70			
11	Duong	Jimmy	60	0	60		50	63	78	67			
12	Francois	Dana	90	95	95		98	87	91	93			
13	Glicksman	Rudy	75	0	70		97	88	92	93			
14	Gondal	Mohammed	85	80	85		87	68	75	55			
15	Harper	Jonathan	70	85	80		87	65	54	87			
16	Jiang	Shirley	80	80	85		93	87	80	75			
17	Khan	Arita	0	60	0		55	45	36	60			
18	Kharkover	Arbiana	75	80	85		87	98	79	83			
19	Kizima	Sofi	85	85	80		73	65	63	71			
20	Lau	Allison	75	80	80		87	54	69	78			
21	Leung	Helen	95	90	95		85	98	98	98			
22	Mattison	Gavin	60	70	65		68	78	78	78			
23	Minauro	Rebekah	50	0	65		65	65	65	65			
24	Mui	Shien	70	65	0		65	70	55	62			
25	Noelus	Gerald	85	80	85		78	87	82	87			
26	Osman	Kennon	90	95	90		90	95	85	47			
27	Rahman	Khubaib	80	90	95		95	100	98	92			
28	Reyes	Kali	90	70	75		78	87	60	69			
29	Sabine	Joseph	75	90	85		98	75	78	87			
30	Shien	Shabbaz	85	90	75		80	65	64	65			
31	Shulovsky	Yulia	90	70	80		78	63	78	78			
32	Skobeleva	Faisal	100	95	95		98	87	91	100			
33	Teo	Diana	75	80	70		65	85	50	78			
34	Wang	Timothy	75	80	75		69	45	36	45			
35	Wong	Liping	80	85	90		78	90	97	98			
36	Xue	Jenny	90	95	100		98	97	87	87			
37	Yan	Zhi Xian	95	100	90		88	98	89	78			
38	Zheng	Dana	80	80	85		78	75	76	87			
39	Zhu	Karl	85	80	80		82	84	86	80			
40													
41	AVERAGE												
42	MAXIMUM												
43	MINIMUM												
44	MODE												
45	MEDIAN												

ACTIVITY 51: NBA® STANDINGS 2

New Skills Reinforced:

In this activity, you will practice how to:

1. expand on the use of the absolute cell reference in formulas.

Activity Overview:

The following activity illustrates how spreadsheets can be used to compute the relationship between the first place team and all the other teams in the division using a formula with an absolute cell reference. An absolute cell reference is used when a reference to a cell's address (either the row, column, or both) must remain fixed. In this activity, you will be using an absolute cell reference to compute the number of "games back" each NBA® team is from the first place team in each division.

This activity expands on the NBA® Standings spreadsheet created in Activity 30.

Instructions:

1. Open the file NBA STANDINGS previously created in Activity 30.

   Note: Unless otherwise stated, the font should be set to Arial, the font size to 10 point.
2. Delete row 1 containing "Activity 30 Student Name."
3. NEW SKILL ▸ Input the formulas for GB (Games Back) for the first place team in each division as follows: (The $ that is used in each formula creates an absolute cell reference to the cells containing the first place team's number of wins in each division.)
   a. In cell E6, type =$B$6-B6

      Use the AutoFill feature to copy the formula down for the remaining teams in the Atlantic Division.
   b. In cell E13, type =$B$13-B13

      Use the AutoFill feature to copy the formula down for the remaining teams in the Central Division.
   c. In cell E20, type =B$20-B20

      Use the AutoFill feature to copy the formula down for the remaining teams in the Southeast Division.
   d. In cell E28, type =$B$28-B28

      Use the AutoFill feature to copy the formula down for the remaining teams in the Northwest Division.
   e. In cell E35, type =$B$35-B35

      Use the AutoFill feature to copy the formula down for the remaining teams in the Pacific Division.
   f. In cell E42, type =$B$42-B42

      Use the AutoFill feature to copy the formula down for the remaining teams in the Southwest Division.

4. Format column E as accounting displaying 0 decimal places and no symbol.
5. Insert a header that shows:
    a. Left Section Activity 51-Student Name
    b. Center Section NBA STANDINGS 2
    c. Right Section Current Date
6. Insert a footer that shows:
    a. Center Section PAGE number
7. Display formulas in your spreadsheet by using <CTRL> + ` to check for accuracy.
8. Carefully proofread your work for accuracy.
9. Save the spreadsheet as NBA STANDINGS 2.
10. Analyze the changes made to the data in the spreadsheet.
11. Set the Print Area to include all cells containing data in the spreadsheet.
12. Print Preview and adjust the Page Setup so that the spreadsheet fits on one page.
13. Print a copy of the spreadsheet if required by your instructor.

	A	B	C	D	E	F	G
1	**N.B.A. STANDINGS**		**2005-2006 Division Standings**				
2							
3							
4	**EASTERN CONFERENCE**						
5	**ATLANTIC DIVISION**	**W**	**L**	**PCT**	**GB**		
6	New Jersey Nets	49	33	0.598			
7	Philadelphia 76ers	38	44	0.463			
8	Boston Celtics	33	49	0.402			
9	Toronto Raptors	27	55	0.329			
10	New York Knicks	23	59	0.280			
11							
12	**CENTRAL DIVISION**	**W**	**L**	**PCT**	**GB**		
13	Detroit Pistons	64	18	0.780			
14	Cleveland Cavaliers	50	32	0.610			
15	Indiana Pacers	41	41	0.500			
16	Chicago Bulls	41	41	0.500			
17	Milwaukee Bucks	40	42	0.488			
18							
19	**SOUTHEAST DIVISION**	**W**	**L**	**PCT**	**GB**		
20	Miami Heat	52	30	0.634			
21	Washington Wizards	42	40	0.512			
22	Orlando Magic	36	46	0.439			
23	Charlotte Bobcats	26	56	0.317			
24	Atlanta Hawks	26	56	0.317			
25							
26	**WESTERN CONFERENCE**						
27	**NORTHWEST DIVISION**	**W**	**L**	**PCT**	**GB**		
28	Denver Nuggets	44	38	0.537			
29	Utah Jazz	41	41	0.500			
30	Seattle SuperSonics	35	47	0.427			
31	Minnesota Timberwolves	33	49	0.402			
32	Portland Trail Blazers	21	61	0.256			
33							
34	**PACIFIC DIVISION**	**W**	**L**	**PCT**	**GB**		
35	Phoenix Suns	54	28	0.659			
36	L.A. Clippers	47	35	0.573			
37	L.A. Lakers	45	37	0.549			
38	Sacramento Kings	44	38	0.537			
39	Golden State Warriors	34	48	0.415			
40							
41	**SOUTHWEST DIVISION**	**W**	**L**	**PCT**	**GB**		
42	San Antonio Spurs	63	19	0.768			
43	Dallas Mavericks	60	22	0.732			
44	Memphis Grizzlies	49	33	0.598			
45	New Orleans Hornets	38	44	0.463			
46	Houston Rockets	34	48	0.415			

ACTIVITY 52: MORTGAGE CALCULATOR

New Skills Reinforced:

In this activity, you will practice how to:

1. use the Payment (PMT) function.

Activity Overview:

Assume that you work for the American Mortgage Co. Your clients constantly want to know how much their monthly mortgage payment will be for different loan amounts. When people apply for a mortgage loan, it is often necessary to calculate the payment to be paid every month for a given period. Knowing how to calculate different mortgages based on varying years and interest rates will help you decide which mortgage is right for your clients based on how much they can afford to pay each month.

In the following activity, you will be using the Payment (PMT) function to compute mortgage payments. The Payment function is used to calculate the payment for a loan based on constant payments and a fixed interest rate.

To use the Payment function, you will need values referenced for the following:

Rate This is the interest rate for the loan.

Nper This is the total number of payments for the loan.

Pv This is the present value, or the total amount that a series of future payments is worth now, also known as the principal.

Instructions:

1. Create a NEW spreadsheet.

   Note: Unless otherwise stated, the font should be set to Arial, the font size to 10 point.
2. Type the data as shown.
3. Bold rows 1 – 15.
4. Change the font size of cell A1 to 16 point.
5. Format the width of columns A – F to 16.0.
6. Format cell C4 as percentages displaying 3 decimal places.
7. NEW SKILL In cell B16, enter the formula =PMT($C$4/12,B$11,-$A16)
8. Select cells B16 – F51 and use the AutoFill feature to copy the formula entered in cell B16 to the remaining cells.
9. Format cells A16 – F51 as currency displaying 2 decimal places and the $ symbol.
10. Right align cells A15 – F51.
11. Format cells B10 – F10 to show a bottom border (as shown in the Data Spreadsheet).
12. Insert a header that shows:
    a. Left Section Activity 52-Student Name
    b. Center Section MORTGAGE CALCULATOR
    c. Right Section Current Date

13. Insert a footer that shows:
    a. Center Section PAGE number
14. Display formulas in your spreadsheet by using <CTRL> + ` to check for accuracy.
15. Carefully proofread your work for accuracy.
16. Save the spreadsheet as MORTGAGE CALCULATOR.
17. Analyze the changes made to the data in the spreadsheet.
18. Set the Print Area to include all cells containing data in the spreadsheet.
19. Print Preview and adjust the Page Setup so that the spreadsheet fits on one page.
20. Print a copy of the spreadsheet if required by your instructor.

ACTIVITY 52: MORTGAGE CALCULATOR DATA SPREADSHEET

	A	B	C	D	E	F
1	American Mortgage Co.					
2	Monthly Payment Table					
3						
4	Percentage Rate:		6.000%			
5						
6			Mortgage In Years			
7						
8		10 Years	15 Years	20 Years	25 Years	30 Years
9		X	X	X	X	X
10		12 Pmts a year	12 Pmts a year	12 Pmts a year	12 Pmts a year	12 Pmts a year
11		120	180	240	300	360
12		Payments	Payments	Payments	Payments	Payments
13						
14						
15	Principal	10 Years	15 Years	20 Years	25 Years	30 Years
16	225000					
17	230000					
18	235000					
19	240000					
20	245000					
21	250000					
22	255000					
23	260000					
24	265000					
25	270000					
26	275000					
27	280000					
28	285000					
29	290000					
30	295000					
31	300000					
32	305000					
33	310000					
34	315000					
35	320000					
36	325000					
37	330000					
38	335000					
39	340000					
40	345000					
41	350000					
42	355000					
43	360000					
44	365000					
45	370000					
46	375000					
47	380000					
48	385000					
49	390000					
50	395000					
51	400000					

ACTIVITY 53: 529 COLLEGE SAVINGS

New Skills Reinforced:

In this activity, you will practice how to:

1. use the Future Value (FV) function.

Activity Overview:

Most parents who save for their children to go to college invest in what is known as a "529 College Savings Plan." If started early enough, a 529 College Savings Plan can yield a solid return. Once a child reaches college, the funds invested in a 529 College Savings Plan can be used to pay for college tuition.

The following activity illustrates how spreadsheets can be used to create a table based upon multiple annuity payments for a college savings fund. To do this, you will be using the Future Value (FV) function. The Future Value function returns the future value of an investment based on periodic, constant payments, and a constant interest rate.

To use the Future Value function, you will need values referenced for the following:

Rate This is the interest rate for the loan.
Nper This is the total number of payments for the loan.
Pv This is the present value or the total amount that a series of future payments is worth now, also known as the principal.

Instructions:

1. Create a NEW spreadsheet.
   Note: Unless otherwise stated, the font should be set to Arial, the font size to 10 point.
2. Type the data as shown.
3. Bold rows 1 – 8.
4. Right align cells B8 – L34.
5. Bold cell A1 and change the font size to 16 point.
6. Format the width of columns A – L to 10.0.
7. NEW SKILL In cell B10, enter the formula =FV($C$3/12,B$8*12,-$A10)
8. Select cells B10 – L34 and use the AutoFill feature to copy the formula entered in cell B10 to the remaining cells.
9. Format cells A10 – L34 as numbers displaying 2 decimal places.
10. Format cell C3 as percents displaying 3 decimal places.
11. Format cells B8 – L8 as numbers displaying 0 decimal places.
12. Insert a header that shows:
    a. Left Section Activity 53-Student Name
    b. Center Section 529 COLLEGE SAVINGS
    c. Right Section Current Date

13. Insert a footer that shows:
    a. Center Section PAGE number
14. Display formulas in your spreadsheet by using <CTRL> + ` to check for accuracy.
15. Carefully proofread your work for accuracy.
16. Save the spreadsheet as 529 COLLEGE SAVINGS.
17. Analyze the changes made to the data in the spreadsheet.
18. Set the Print Area to include all cells containing data in the spreadsheet.
19. Print Preview and adjust the Page Setup so that the spreadsheet fits on one page. Set the page orientation to landscape.
20. Print a copy of the spreadsheet if required by your instructor.

ACTIVITY 53: 529 COLLEGE SAVINGS DATA SPREADSHEET

	A	B	C	D	E	F	G	H	I	J	K	L
1	529 COLLEGE SAVINGS CALCULATOR											
2												
3	Percentage Rate:		5.000%									
4												
5												
6	Payment				College Savings In Years							
7	per											
8	Month	8	9	10	11	12	13	14	15	16	17	18
9												
10	50											
11	55											
12	60											
13	65											
14	70											
15	75											
16	80											
17	85											
18	90											
19	95											
20	100											
21	105											
22	110											
23	115											
24	120											
25	125											
26	130											
27	135											
28	140											
29	145											
30	150											
31	155											
32	160											
33	165											
34	166.67											

ACTIVITY 54: NFL® FANTASY FOOTBALL®

New Skills Reinforced:

In this activity, you will practice how to:

1. use the ROUNDDOWN function.

Activity Overview:

Fantasy Football® is a game played by football fans in which participants draft their own team and compete with teams built by others. Fantasy Football® allows fans to take an active, personal role in professional football, therefore increasing their enjoyment of the game. The fans get to create their own roster of players by drafting talent from actual NFL® teams. Leagues are usually formed with 10-14 of these fans, who become the owners/ managers of their own unique roster. A draft is held, where all the league members get together with each other and draft 14-20 NFL players. At the end of the season, one owner emerges as the champion. Fantasy Football® has been played for over 20 years, with an estimated six to eight million fans involved.

The following activity illustrates how spreadsheets can be used to calculate the points for the top fantasy players in the 2005 NFL® season.

Instructions:

1. Create a NEW spreadsheet.
   Note: Unless otherwise stated, the font should be set to Arial, the font size to 10 point.
2. Type the data as shown.
3. Format the width of columns A – C to 20.0 and left align.
4. Bold cell A1 and change the font size to 16 point.
5. Bold row 4.
6. Bold cells A5, A14, and A24.
7. Center align columns D, E, and F.
8. Compute the PTS (Points) in each position. Since decimals are not allowed in the NFL Fantasy Football® scoring system, the ROUNDDOWN function is required to round the answers to the formulas down to the nearest whole number. The formulas for the first player in each position are given below.

   NEW SKILL

   a. **QUARTERBACKS:** *Every 20 yards of passing=1 point; every touchdown pass=2 points*
      PTS=(YARDS/20)+(TDS*2) -> In cell F5, type =ROUNDDOWN(((D5/20)+(E5*2)),0)
   b. **RUNNING BACKS:** *Every 10 yards rushing=1 point; every touchdown scored=4 points*
      PTS=(YARDS/10)+(TDS*4) -> In cell F14, type =ROUNDDOWN(((D14/10)+(E14*4)),0)
   c. **WIDE RECEIVERS:** *Every 8 yards of receiving=1 point; every touchdown caught=5 points*
      PTS=(YARDS/8)+(TDS*5) -> In cell F24, type =ROUNDDOWN(((D24/8)+(E24*5)),0)
9. Use the AutoFill feature to copy the formulas for the remaining players in each position.

10. Insert a header that shows:
    a. Left Section Activity 54-Student Name
    b. Center Section NFL FANTASY FOOTBALL
    c. Right Section Current Date
11. Insert a footer that shows:
    a. Center Section PAGE number
12. Display formulas in your spreadsheet by using <CTRL> + ` to check for accuracy.
13. Carefully proofread your work for accuracy.
14. Save the spreadsheet as NFL FANTASY FOOTBALL.
15. Analyze the changes made to the data in the spreadsheet.
16. Set the Print Area to include all cells containing data in the spreadsheet.
17. Print Preview and adjust the Page Setup so that the spreadsheet fits on one page.
18. Print a copy of the spreadsheet if required by your instructor.

ACTIVITY 54: NFL® FANTASY FOOTBALL® DATA SPREADSHEET

	A	B	C	D	E	F
1	NFL FANTASY FOOTBALL 2005 STATISTICS					
2						
3						
4	POSITION	PLAYER	TEAM	YARDS	TDS	PTS
5	QUARTERBACKS	Tom Brady	Patriots	4110	26	
6		Trent Green	Chiefs	4014	17	
7		Carson Palmer	Bengals	3836	32	
8		Eli Manning	Giants	3762	24	
9		Peyton Manning	Colts	3747	28	
10		Drew Brees	Chargers	3639	23	
11		Matt Hasselback	Seahawks	3459	24	
12						
13						
14	RUNNING BACKS	Shaun Alexander	Seahawks	1880	27	
15		Tiki Barber	Giants	1860	9	
16		Larry Johnson	Chiefs	1750	20	
17		Clinton Portis	Redskins	1516	11	
18		Edgerrin James	Colts	1506	13	
19		LaDanian Tomlinson	Chargers	1462	18	
20		Rudi Johnson	Bengals	1458	12	
21						
22						
23						
24	WIDE RECEIVERS	Steve Smith	Panthers	1563	12	
25		Santana Moss	Redskins	1483	9	
26		Chad Johnson	Bengals	1432	9	
27		Larry Fitzgerald	Cardinals	1409	10	
28		Anquan Boldon	Cardinals	1402	7	
29		Tory Holt	Rams	1331	9	
30		Marvin Harrison	Colts	1146	12	

Source: www.fantasyfootball.com

ACTIVITY 55: COMPUTER GAMES

New Skills Reinforced:

In this activity, you will practice how to:
1. rename worksheets
2. use multiple worksheets.
3. create Paste Link formulas that link data in multiple worksheets.

Activity Overview:

A computer-role playing game, or RPG, is a genre of games in which a player assumes the role and actions of a character. Strategy skills, team-building, and imagination are all part of this type of game. The game is played using a predefined collection of rules. The popularity of RPGs for video games has grown tremendously over the last decade. Gamers of all ages find these games enjoyable causing sales to skyrocket when a new game is released.

The following activity illustrates how spreadsheets can be used to record the sales activity of top selling RPG games for a retail video game store.

Instructions:

1. Create a NEW spreadsheet.

   Note: Unless otherwise stated, the font should be set to Arial, the font size to 10 point.

NEW SKILL 2. Rename Sheet 1 in the spreadsheet as TOP 5 RPG.

3. Rename Sheet 2 in the spreadsheet as MARCH 2006 SALES.

NEW SKILL **Instructions for the TOP 5 RPG Worksheet:**

1. Type the data as shown.
2. Format the width of column A to 6.0 and left align.
3. Format the width of column B to 37.0 and left align.
4. Format the width of column C to 11.0 and left align.
5. Format the width of column D to 11.0 and center align.
6. Format cells D5 – D9 as currency displaying 2 decimal places and the $ symbol.
7. Format the width of column E to 16.0 and left align.
8. Format the width of column F to 7.0 and left align.
9. Format the width of column G to 12.0, right align, and as dates displaying mm/dd/yy.
10. To avoid losing data, save the spreadsheet as COMPUTER GAMES.

NEW SKILL **Instructions for the MARCH 2006 SALES Worksheet:**

1. Type the data as shown.
2. Format the width of column A to 37.0 and left align.
3. Format the width of column B to 11.0 and center align.
4. Format cells B5 – B9 as currency displaying 2 decimal places and the $ symbol.
5. Format the width of column C to 12.0 and center align.
6. Format cells C5 – C9 as numbers displaying 0 decimal places.
7. Format the width of column D to 15.0 and center align.
8. Format cells D5 – D9 as currency displaying 2 decimal places and the $ symbol.

NEW SKILL
9. Complete the data in column A, Title, by entering the following Paste Link formula to copy the data from Column B, Title, in the TOP 5 RPG worksheet:

    In cell A5, type ='TOP 5 RPG'!B5
10. Use the AutoFill feature to copy the formula down for the remaining Titles.

NEW SKILL
11. Complete the data in column B, List Price, by entering the following Paste Link formula to copy the data from column D, List Price, in the TOP 5 RPG worksheet:

    In cell B5, type ='TOP 5 RPG'!D5
12. Use the AutoFill feature to copy the formula down for the remaining List Prices.
13. Enter formulas to compute the Total Sales (in column D) for each game.

    Total Sales=List Price*# of Units Sold -> In cell D5, type =B5*C5
14. Use the AutoFill feature to copy the formula down for the remaining Total Sales.

Instructions for both the TOP 5 RPG and MARCH 2006 SALES Worksheets:

1. Insert a header on each worksheet that shows:
    a. Left Section — Activity 55-Student Name
    b. Center Section — COMPUTER GAMES
    c. Right Section — Current Date
2. Insert a footer on each worksheet that shows:
    a. Center Section — PAGE number
3. Display formulas in both worksheets by using <CTRL> + ` to check for accuracy.
4. Carefully proofread your work for accuracy.
5. Save the spreadsheet.
6. Analyze the changes made to the data in the spreadsheet.
7. Set the Print Area to include all cells containing data in both worksheets.
8. Print Preview and adjust the Page Setup so that both worksheets each fit on one page.
9. Print a copy of both worksheets if required by your instructor.

ACTIVITY 55: COMPUTER GAMES DATA SPREADSHEET

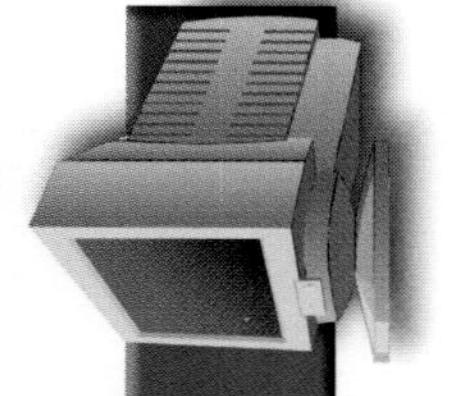

TOP 5 RPG Sheet 1

	A	B	C	D	E	F	G
1	Don's Computer Games						
2	Top 5 Role Playing Games (RPG)						
3							
4	Rank	Title	Platform	List Price	Manufacturer	Rating	Release Date
5	1	Elder Scrolls 4: Oblivion	Windows XP	$49.99	Take 2	Teen	3/20/06
6	2	Elder Scrolls 4: Oblivion Collector's Edition	Windows 98	$59.99	2K Games	Teen	3/20/06
7	3	Guild Wars Factions	Windows XP	$49.99	NC Interactive	Teen	4/28/06
8	4	Final Fantasy XI: Treasures of Aht Urhgan	Windows XP	$29.99	Square Enix USA	Teen	4/18/06
9	5	World of Warcraft	Macintosh	$49.99	Vivendi Universal	Teen	11/23/04

MARCH 2006 SALES Sheet 2

	A	B	C	D
1	Don's Computer Games			
2	Monthly Sales for March 2006			
3				
4	Title	List Price	# of Units Sold	Total Sales
5			200	
6			150	
7			75	
8			50	
9			20	

Source: http://www.marked4sale.com/computer_games.htm

ACTIVITY 56: COMIC BOOKS

New Skills Reinforced:

In this activity, you will practice how to:
1. create an exploded pie chart.

Activity Overview:

Some say that there is a comic book out there for everyone. Comic book collecting is a very popular hobby that drives the comic book industry sales. Readers will pay top dollar for a rare comic book and will try to invest in currently printed books at the best price to insure a greater return in years to come. A resource like Comics Buyer's Guide is a great place to go for information about pricing and reviews of comic books. They also track sales information from the world's leading comic book distributor, Diamond Comic Distributors.

The following activity illustrates how spreadsheets can be used to graphically illustrate the estimated sales of popular comic books.

Instructions:

1. Create a NEW spreadsheet.

   Note: Unless otherwise stated, the font should be set to Arial, the font size to 10 point.
2. Type the data as shown.
3. Use the AutoFill feature to finish the numbering sequence in cells A5 – A24.
4. Format the width of column A to 6.0.
5. Adjust the width of columns B – F using the AutoFit feature.
6. Bold cells A1 and A2 and change the font size to 16 point.
7. Bold row 4.
8. Format cells C5 – C24 as text and center align.
9. Format columns D and F as currency displaying 2 decimal places and the $ symbol.

NEW SKILL

10. Create an exploded pie chart as follows:
    a. Select cells B4 – B24 and F4 – F24 simultaneously.
    b. Using the Chart Wizard, select Pie for the Chart type and Pie with a 3-D visual effect for the Chart sub-type.
    c. Set the pie chart to Series in Columns.
    d. Enter the chart title as ESTIMATED SALES.
    e. Display the legend at the bottom of the pie chart.
    f. Show no data labels.
    g. Save the chart as a new sheet. Name the new sheet COMIC BOOKS CHART.
11. Format the style of the pie chart as follows:
    a. Select the largest piece of the pie chart (Infinite Crisis) and drag the piece out (explode it) to add emphasis.
    b. Format the exploded piece's data point to show the data label's value.
12. When formatted, your pie chart should look similar to the one provided in Figure 1-56.

13. Insert a header for both the spreadsheet and the chart that shows:
    a. Left Section Activity 56-Student Name
    b. Center Section COMIC BOOKS
    c. Right Section Current Date
14. Insert a footer that shows:
    a. Center Section PAGE number
15. Carefully proofread your work for accuracy.
16. Save the spreadsheet as COMIC BOOKS.
17. Analyze the changes made to the data in the spreadsheet.
18. Print Preview and adjust the Page Setup so that the spreadsheet and chart each fit on one page. Set the page orientation to landscape for the chart.
19. Print a copy of the spreadsheet and chart if required by your instructor.

ACTIVITY 56: COMIC BOOKS DATA SPREADSHEET

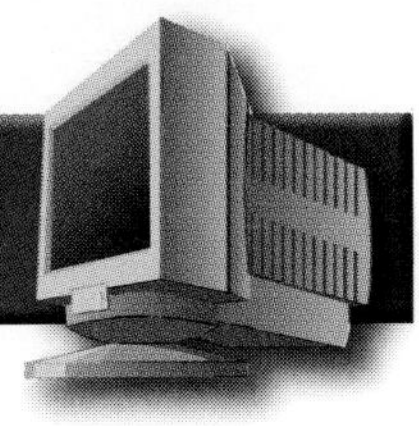

	A	B	C	D	E	F
1	March 2006 Comic Book Orders					
2	from Diamond Comic Distributors					
3						
4		Comic Book Title	Issue	Price	Publisher	Est. sales
5	1	Infinite Crisis	5	3.99	DC	201800
6	2	New Avengers	17	2.5	Marvel	121100
7		All Star Superman	3	2.99	DC	110600
8		New Avengers Illuminati Sp	N/A	3.99	Marvel	107900
9		Superman Batman	24 (Res)	2.99	DC	101300
10		Ultimates 2	10	2.99	Marvel	94900
11		Amazing Spider-Man	530	2.5	Marvel	89900
12		Green Lantern	10	2.99	DC	79700
13		Uncanny X-Men	470	2.5	Marvel	79400
14		Infinite Crisis Secret Files 2006		5.99	DC	78700
15		Uncanny X-Men	471	2.5	Marvel	78300
16		X-Men	184	2.5	Marvel	78000
17		Ultimate Extinction	3	2.99	Marvel	75800
18		Wolverine	40	2.99	Marvel	75500
19		X-Men Deadly Genesis	5	3.5	Marvel	74700
20		Ultimate Spider-Man	91	2.5	Marvel	74000
21		Ms Marvel	1	2.99	Marvel	73400
22		Ultimate X-Men	68	2.5	Marvel	72800
23		Ultimate Spider-Man	92	2.5	Marvel	72300
24		Batman	651	2.5	DC	69800

Source: http://www.cbgxtra.com/Default.aspx?tabid=1642

Note: The chart for this activity is shown on the next page.

Figure 1-56

ESTIMATED SALES

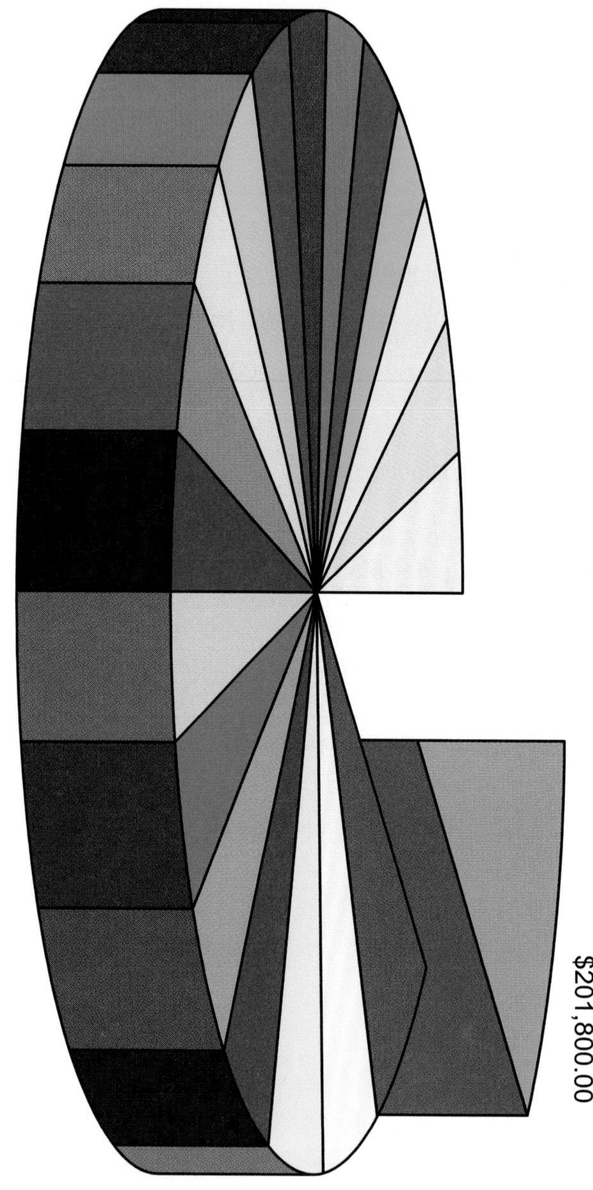

ACTIVITY 57: WHO GOT PUNK'D®?

New Skills Reinforced:

In this activity, you will practice how to:

1. combine cells in a spreadsheet.

Activity Overview:

Assume you are a writer for the entertainment section of your school's newspaper. The editor of the newspaper has asked you to research and write an article about the reality TV show Punk'D®, which airs on MTV®. Punk'D®, which is hosted by Ashton Kutcher, has drawn in millions of viewers since its debut season in 2003.

In Punk'D®, Kutcher pulls outrageous pranks on celebrities for the audiences' viewing pleasure. As part of your research in writing the article for the newspaper, you decide to use a spreadsheet to keep a list of some of the most popular celebrities who have been "Punk'D" on the show.

The following activity illustrates how to combine data entered in separate cells.

Instructions:

1. Create a NEW spreadsheet.

   Note: Unless otherwise stated, the font should be set to Arial, the font size to 10 point.
2. Type the data as shown.
3. Bold cell A1 and change the font size to 16 point.
4. Format the width of column A to 16.0, column B to 14.0, and column C to 22.0.
5. Left align columns A – C.
6. Bold row 3.
7. NEW SKILL Enter a formula to combine the text in cells for the FIRST NAME and LAST NAME as follows:

   In cell C4, type =A4&" "&B4

   (The first and last names should now be combined into one cell)
8. Use the AutoFill feature to copy the formula down for the remaining names.
9. Fill cells C3 – C22 with the color yellow.
10. Insert a header that shows:
    a. Left Section Activity 57-Student Name
    b. Center Section WHO GOT PUNK'D?
    c. Right Section Current Date
11. Insert a footer that shows:
    a. Center Section PAGE number
12. Display formulas in your spreadsheet by using <CTRL> + ` to check for accuracy.
13. Carefully proofread your work for accuracy.
14. Save the spreadsheet as WHO GOT PUNK'D.
15. Analyze the changes made to the data in the spreadsheet.
16. Set the Print Area to include all cells containing data in the spreadsheet.
17. Print Preview and adjust the Page Setup so that the spreadsheet fits on one page.
18. Print a copy of the spreadsheet if required by your instructor.

ACTIVITY 57: WHO GOT PUNK'D®? DATA SPREADSHEET

	A	B	C
1	Who Got Punk'D?		
2			
3	FIRST NAME	LAST NAME	FULL NAME
4	Jon	Abrahams	
5	Christina	Aguilera	
6	Tori	Amos	
7	Pamela	Anderson	
8	Christina	Applegate	
9	Tom	Arnold	
10	Kory	Bassett	
11	Jerome	Bettis	
12	Jessica	Biel	
13	Pierce	Brosnan	
14	Nick	Lachey	
15	Frankie	Muniz	
16	Jack	Osbourne	
17	Kelly	Osbourne	
18	Kid	Rock	
19	Jessica	Simpson	
20	Britney	Spears	
21	Justin	Timberlake	
22	Wilmer	Valderrama	

ACTIVITY 58: MONTHLY CALENDAR

New Skills Reinforced:

In this activity, you will practice how to:

1. use a spreadsheet to create a monthly calendar.

Activity Overview:

Spreadsheets are very powerful tools to use for calculating and organizing data. However, spreadsheets can also be used to create a variety of other useful documents including weekly, monthly, and yearly calendars.

The following activity illustrates how a spreadsheet can be used to create a monthly calendar.

Instructions:

1. Create a NEW spreadsheet.

   Note: Unless otherwise stated, the font should be set to Arial, the font size to 10 point.
2. Type the data as shown.
3. Bold cell A1 and change the font size to 20 point.
4. Format the width of columns A – G to 24.0. (**Hint:** You may wish to reduce the zoom percentage on your screen so that you can view all of the columns.)
5. Format the height of row 3 to 20.0.
6. Format the height of rows 4, 6, 8, 10, and 12 to 13.0.
7. Format the height of rows 5, 7, 9, 11, and 13 to 100.0.
8. Bold row 3 and center align.
9. Right align cells A4 – G13.
10. Change the fill color to 25% gray for cells A4 – G4, A6 – G6, A8 – G8, A10 – G10, and A12 – C12.
11. Insert a header that shows:
    a. Left Section	Activity 58-Student Name
    b. Center Section	MONTHLY CALENDAR
    c. Right Section	Current Date
12. Carefully proofread your work for accuracy.
13. Save the spreadsheet as MONTHLY CALENDAR.
14. Set the Print Area to include cells A1 – G13.
15. Print Preview and adjust the Page Setup so that the spreadsheet fits on one page. Set the left, right, top, and bottom margins to .25 inches. Set the page to center horizontally and vertically. Set the page orientation to landscape. Set the page to print gridlines.
16. Print a copy of the spreadsheet if required by your instructor.

ACTIVITY 58: MONTHLY CALENDAR DATA SPREADSHEET

	A	B	C	D	E	F	G
1	January 2007						
2							
3	Monday	Tuesday	Wednesday	Thursday	Friday	Saturday	Sunday
4	1	2	3	4	5	6	7
5							
6	8	9	10	11	12	13	14
7							
8	15	16	17	18	19	20	21
9							
10	22	23	24	25	26	27	28
11							
12	29	30	31				
13							

ACTIVITY 59: PROM EXPENSES

New Skills Reinforced:

In this activity, you will practice how to:

1. format a business letter using Microsoft Word.
2. insert an Excel spreadsheet into a Microsoft Word document.

Activity Overview:

Assume that you are the secretary of your school's student council. One of your jobs is to keep students informed about upcoming events. One upcoming event at your school is the senior prom. To help your fellow classmates prepare for the expenses involved with the prom, you are asked to prepare a letter addressed to each member of your class.

The following activity illustrates how a Microsoft Excel® spreadsheet can be integrated with a Microsoft Word® document.

Instructions:

1. Create a NEW document in Microsoft Word. Type the document in Times New Roman font and with a font size of 12 point.
2. Set the left and right margins to 1 inch, top to 1.5 inches, and bottom to .5 inches.
3. NEW SKILL ▸ Type the text shown in the business letter provided. Stop typing when you reach the end of the first paragraph in the body of the letter.
4. Create and insert the Microsoft Excel Worksheet located under the first paragraph in the letter by following the instructions provided below.

NEW SKILL ▸ **Instructions for creating the Microsoft Excel Worksheet inside the letter:**

a. Position the cursor two lines below the first paragraph in the letter.
b. From the "Insert" menu, choose "Object" then "Microsoft Excel Worksheet."
c. Type the data as shown in the spreadsheet provided.
   Note: Unless otherwise stated, the font should be set to Arial, the font size to 10 point.
d. Bold cell A1 and change the font size to 14 point.
e. Bold and underline cells A3 – D4.
f. Format the width of column A to 18.0, column B to 11.0, column C to 13.0, and column D to 9.0.
g. Format cells B5 – D10 as currency displaying 0 decimal places and the $ symbol.
h. Left align columns A – D.
i. Enter formulas to compute the totals for columns B and D.
j. Bold cells A10 – D10.
k. Underline cells B9 and D9.
l. Center align the Excel Worksheet in the letter.

5. Type the remainder of the letter as shown in the business letter provided.
6. Type your name for the student's name.
7. Carefully proofread your work for accuracy.
8. Save the Word document as PROM EXPENSES.
9. Print a copy of the Word document if required by your instructor.

<Current Date>

Alicia Hanon
Graduate of the Class of 2007
8558 Naomi Avenue
Portland, ME 04101

Dear Alicia:

To help you prepare and budget for our upcoming prom, the student council has researched prom expenses for this year, and we wanted to share the information with you. Below, you will see a list of prom-related expenses for both girls and guys. We hope this helps make your planning a little easier.

	A	B	C	D
1	PROM-RELATED EXPENSES			
2				
3	GIRL'S		BOY'S	
4	EXPENSES	AMOUNT	EXPENSES	AMOUNT
5	Ticket	75	Ticket	75
6	Dress	250	Tuxedo	100
7	Boutonniere	15	Corsage	50
8	Photographs	35	Photographs	35
9	Limousine	200	Limousine	200
10	TOTALS			

Insert an Excel spreadsheet here

We look forward to seeing you at the prom this year. We know it will be the best this school has ever had!

Sincerely,

Student's Name
Student Council Secretary

ACTIVITY 60: COLLEGE CHOICES

New Skills Reinforced:

In this activity, you will practice how to:

1. use a spreadsheet as a database to store and organize data.

Activity Overview:

Going to college will be one of the biggest decisions you will ever make. Many factors have to be considered and researched to ensure that the college you choose to attend is "right for you." Among these factors, location, tuition costs, and your decided major are the most important.

In this activity, you will use a spreadsheet to create a database of ten possible colleges you can attend.

Instructions:

1. Create a NEW spreadsheet.
   Note: Unless otherwise stated, the font should be set to Arial, the font size to 10 point.
2. Type the data as shown.
3. Access the Internet and use a popular search engine such as Google or Yahoo! to research ten possible colleges and/or technical or trade schools you would consider attending after graduating from high school.
4. NEW SKILL ▶ Type the information you have researched into the spreadsheet as follows:
   a. Column A: Type the NAME of the school
   b. Column B: Type the CITY of the school
   c. Column C: Type the STATE of the school
   d. Column D: Type the TUITION COST of the school
   e. Column E: Type the WEB SITE ADDRESS of the school
   f. Column F: Choose the top three schools you would like to attend. Indicate your top three choices by typing "First Choice," "Second Choice," and "Third Choice," respectively, in the "MY TOP 3 CHOICES" column.
5. Adjust the widths of columns A – F so that the data fits in each cell.
6. Format the fonts, styles, and cell colors to enhance the look of the spreadsheet.
7. Sort the spreadsheet by TUITION COST in descending order (Z–A).
8. Insert a header that shows:
   a. Left Section Activity 60-Student Name
   b. Center Section COLLEGE CHOICES
   c. Right Section Current Date
9. Insert a footer that shows:
   a. Center Section PAGE number
10. Carefully proofread your work for accuracy.
11. Save the spreadsheet as COLLEGE CHOICES.

12. Analyze the changes made to the data in the spreadsheet.
13. Set the Print Area to include all cells containing data in the spreadsheet.
14. Print Preview and adjust the Page Setup so that the spreadsheet fits on one page.
15. Print a copy of the spreadsheet if required by your instructor.

ACTIVITY 60: COLLEGE CHOICES DATA SPREADSHEET

	A	B	C	D	E	F
1	MY COLLEGE CHOICES					
2						
3	NAME	CITY	STATE	TUITION COST	WEB SITE ADDRESS	MY TOP 3 CHOICES